slow cooking
for
vegetarians

annette yates

foulsham
LONDON • NEW YORK • TORONTO • SYDNEY

foulsham

The Publishing House, Bennetts Close, Cippenham, Slough,
Berkshire, SL1 5AP, England

Foulsham books can be found in all good bookshops and direct from
www.foulsham.com

ISBN: 978–0–572–03387–3

Previously published as *Real Food Vegetarian Recipes for your Slo-cooker*

Other books for your slow cooker:
Slow Cooking from Around the World (978-0-572-03289-0)
New Recipes for Your Slo-cooker (978-0-572-02636-3)
Real Food from Your Slo-cooker (978-0-572-02536-6)
Slow Cooking for Yourself (978-0-572-03150-3)
Slow Cooking from Around the Mediterranean (978-0-572-03323-1)

Printed in Great Britain by Mackays Ltd, Chatham, Kent

slow cooking
for
vegetarians

18

CONTENTS

ACKNOWLEDGEMENTS

The recipes in this book were tested in a range of slow cookers. I am particularly indebted to Haden and Morphy Richards for their generosity in supplying the latest models.

Thanks, too, must go to my editor, Gill Holloway, for spotting all the errors and omissions in my manuscript and for making my text clear and readable!

INTRODUCTION

Eating meals without meat or fish is no longer regarded as wacky, out of the ordinary or an exercise in self-denial. In fact, millions of people in the UK today lean towards a diet that is partially or entirely vegetarian.

I will come clean right now – I am not a vegetarian. I just love vegetables. I still enjoy meat in small quantities and fish at least twice a week, but more and more I am aware that I am choosing meals that are made up entirely of vegetables, rice and grains. Not only that, but I often find that my friends and family also prefer to opt for dishes without meat or fish.

These days I find that, like so many other people, I have less and less time to spend on actual cooking. As a result I tend to opt for dishes that can be assembled in minutes and either require minimal cooking time or can be left to cook gently and slowly for hours while I am busy doing other things. And this is where the slow cooker comes in really handy.

A slow cooker is, quite simply, a casserole powered by an electric element that uses no more energy than a lightbulb. It can be left to cook your meal, day or night, and the long, gentle cooking means that wonderfully complex flavours develop and there is little or no risk of the food drying out. You can slow-cook every kind of dish, from soups to cakes and puddings, and there are many dishes that are ideal for making in a slow cooker, even though they may cook in a relatively short time (say in an hour or two). The advantages are that rather than switch on the oven – expensive – or stand over the hob – time-consuming – you can simply leave the food to cook on its own, saving you both money and time.

This is not a book about how to be a vegetarian or how to use a slow cooker per se. It is simply a collection of delicious recipes for your slow cooker that just happen to be vegetarian – slow cooking married with vegetarian eating. The dishes I've chosen are those that have been appreciated by my family and friends, vegetarian and meat-eaters alike. I hope you will enjoy them too.

Do note that many of the recipes contain dairy products and so are not suitable for vegans. They can, however, be easily adapted by substituting the many vegetarian alternatives, such as soya milk and cream and vegetarian cheeses, that are readily available in supermarkets.

This book is also for those readers of my title *New Recipes for Your Slo-cooker* who have contacted me for advice and ideas on cooking vegetarian dishes. All the recipes are brand new except the one for Christmas pudding, which is simply too good to improve.

Happy (slow) cooking!

GETTING THE BEST OUT OF YOUR SLOW COOKER

There are many different makes of slow cooker and they come in a wide range of shapes and sizes. Your manufacturer's instruction booklet is the best guide for using your particular slow cooker, so do check with it regularly.

Getting started

- All slow cookers have at least two settings, High and Low. The Low setting cooks very slowly with only gentle simmering – this is particularly suitable for casseroles and custard puddings. On the High setting, food is cooked at a higher temperature and any liquid bubbles constantly – ideal if you want to speed up the meal, and perfect for cooking puddings and cakes that contain raising agents. Some slow cookers have an Auto-cook function – this starts cooking on High, then automatically switches to Low for the remainder of the cooking time (this is very useful if you need to put all the ingredients in cold).

- The cooking time on Low is generally just over twice that on High.

- Though it's not always necessary, I usually switch on the slow cooker and preheat it on High while I am preparing the ingredients. Always check with your manufacturer's instruction book to see what it recommends. Preheating is essential if you plan to put all the ingredients in cold and then cook on the Low setting. It is also important when steaming puddings. Always preheat on High with the lid on.

- You can adapt conventional recipes for use in your slow cooker. The table on page 10 gives a general guide to calculating cooking times.

Conventional cooking time	Cooking time in a slow cooker		
	Low	High	Auto
30 minutes	6–8 hours	3–4 hours	5–7 hours
30 minutes–1 hour	8–10 hours	5–6 hours	6–8 hours
1–3 hours	10–12 hours	7–8 hours	8–10 hours

- When adapting conventional recipes for slow cooking, use about half the quantity of liquid in the recipe.

Preparing ingredients for slow cooking

- Thaw frozen foods before adding them to the slow cooker. Frozen vegetables need less cooking than fresh and are best added to the slow cooker towards the end of the cooking time – usually only for the final 30 minutes.
- Cut root vegetables (see page 14) into even-sized pieces and push them down into the cooking liquid to encourage even and thorough cooking.
- I usually soften onions and root vegetables on the hob before adding them to the slow cooker. Not only does this improve the appearance, texture and flavour of the finished dish, it also helps to raise the temperature of the vegetables to a point where they can begin to cook. However, if you do not have time for this, you can usually put all the ingredients in cold but remember that the cooking time will be longer.
- Soak dried beans in plenty of cold water before slow cooking (see page 16). Red kidney beans should be boiled rapidly for 10 minutes before being added.
- Use 'easy-cook' rice for best results and rinse it first.
- Do not be tempted to leave prepared raw ingredients in the slow cooker for cooking later. Store them in the fridge until you are ready to start cooking.
- Season sparingly before cooking – flavours are concentrated in the slow cooker, so it's best to adjust the seasoning to taste towards the end of the cooking time.
- Thickening agents can be added either at the start or near the end of cooking. For instance, if you are softening vegetables on the hob, stir in some flour before adding the cooking liquid and bringing to the boil. If you prefer to season at the end of cooking, blend a little flour or cornflour (cornstarch) with cold water to make a smooth paste and

stir into the slow cooker 30 minutes to 1 hour before the end of cooking.

- Your slow cooker will work best if it is at least one-quarter full, up to a maximum of 2.5 cm/1 in from the top (check with your manufacturer's instruction book).
- Always make sure there is some liquid in the slow cooker during cooking.

During cooking

- Resist the temptation to lift the lid and peep during cooking. This will cause a marked drop in temperature, slowing down the cooking process. For each time you open the lid, you will need to add 15–30 minutes to the total cooking time.
- If the food is not cooked after the recommended time, switch the slow cooker to High and cook for a further 30 minutes to 1 hour.
- To prevent milk and cream separating during cooking, they are usually best added to the slow cooker for only the final 30 minutes of cooking.
- Pasta and rice are best added to soups and casseroles for the final 30 minutes of cooking.
- On rare occasions when food in the slow cooker may have become over-dry or too thick (maybe because you arrive home much later than planned), you can add extra hot liquid, such as water or stock. Always switch off the power before you pour it in.
- When cooking cakes and puddings, check that the dish or basin you intend to use will fit comfortably in the slow cooker with the lid on.
- When a dish is cooked and you want to keep it warm, switch the slow cooker to the Low setting. The food may need stirring occasionally to prevent its surface from drying out.
- If your slow cooker has a removable pot, you can put it under the grill (broiler) or in the oven to brown any toppings you have added. Check your manufacturer's instruction booklet for details.

Care and hygiene

- Do not store cooked food in the slow cooker. Any leftover food should be transferred to a container to cool completely, then chilled in the fridge or frozen.
- Do not reheat cooked food in the slow cooker – it is too slow and the temperature is not high enough to kill any bacteria.
- Look after your slow cooker and it will give you years of reliable service. Follow the manufacturer's advice for cleaning and care.

VEGETABLES IN YOUR SLOW COOKER

This section provides a brief guide to the best vegetables to choose for cooking in your slow cooker, how to prepare them and what to watch out for.

Note that as well as fresh vegetables, you can use frozen and canned vegetables if you prefer. Frozen vegetables should always be thawed completely before adding to the slow cooker or they will lower the temperature and extend the cooking time. Stir them in during the final 30 minutes to 1 hour of cooking.

All types of canned vegetables are suitable for adding to slow-cooked recipes. They will only require a short cooking time, so can be added just for the last 30 minutes to 1 hour.

Garlic, leeks, onions, shallots

I would find it very difficult to do without this group of vegetables. They form the basis of most savoury recipes, adding their wonderful flavours and a certain sweetness to dishes.

Garlic: I prefer to chop garlic finely but you can crush it (either with a knife on a board or in a garlic crusher) if you prefer. It may then be added to the dish at the start of cooking or used as a garnish with lemon zest and parsley as in Gremolata (see page 82).

Leeks: These are lovely in soups, sauces and casseroles. They should be thinly sliced and added at the start of cooking.

Onions: These may be white, brown, yellow or red. They should be finely chopped or thinly sliced. Like root vegetables (see next page), onions and leeks need to reach a reasonably high temperature before they can begin to cook. Since this is not always possible in a slow cooker, I usually soften them first (and sometimes brown them too) in a little oil or butter before adding them to the slow cooker.

Shallots: These can be casseroled whole. If they are sliced or chopped, they are best softened in oil or butter on the hob before being added to the rest of the ingredients.

Spring onions (scallions): Slice these before adding to the slow cooker. They retain their texture and flavour better if they are added only for the final 20–30 minutes of cooking.

Root vegetables

This group includes beetroot (red beets), carrots, celeriac (celery root), Jerusalem artichokes, parsnips, potatoes, sweet potatoes, swedes (rutabaga), turnips and yams.

Each has its own distinctive, earthy flavour. All are delicious in soups and casseroles and all are ideal for long, slow cooking. Like onions, they need to reach quite a high temperature before they can start to cook, so before adding them to the slow cooker, it's best to soften even-sized pieces in a little oil or butter, then add the cooking liquid and bring the whole lot to the boil. To make sure they cook evenly, push the vegetables down into the liquid so they will be immersed during cooking.

Aubergines, chillies, peppers and tomatoes

Although these are actually fruit, we tend to class them as vegetables.

Aubergines (eggplants): These soften beautifully in the slow cooker, adding their creamy texture to all kind of dishes. Cut them into even-sized pieces and cook gently in some olive oil on the hob to soften and brown, before adding to the slow cooker.

Chillies: These may be yellow, green, red and black. They may be used whole, sliced or chopped to add flavour, colour and heat to many dishes. It is worth remembering that the smaller chillies are usually the hottest and that the heat lies in the seeds and white membrane – so if you want a milder dish, remove these before adding the pod to the other ingredients in the slow cooker. As well as fresh, you can buy them dried, crushed, as powder, paste and in sauces, and all are useful for adding to dishes.

(Bell) peppers: These are available in beautiful colours. The flavour varies from the slight bitterness of green, white and black to the warm sweetness of yellow, orange and red, but all have a mild flavour and juicy flesh. With their tops cut off and the seeds removed, they can be stuffed and cooked whole. Alternatively, you can slice or dice them and add them to soups and casseroles to become meltingly tender. If you want the pieces to retain some 'bite', add to the slow cooker for only the final 30–40 minutes of cooking.

Jars and cans of softened or roasted peppers are a useful standby and can be drained and added to ingredients in the slow cooker.

Tomatoes: To my mind, these are almost as useful as onions – in my cooking anyway. Fresh tomatoes can be chopped and mixed with other ingredients in your slow cooker. Plum tomatoes tend to have the best flavour. Cherry tomatoes are sweet and are best added near the end of cooking so that they retain their shape. Canned tomatoes (whole, chopped or cherry) are very versatile and can form the basis of many soups, sauces and casseroles in the slow cooker. Dried tomatoes have a chewy texture with an intense flavour and are usually supplied dry or packed in oil – chop them and stir into the slow cooker at the start of cooking. I particularly like to use semi-dried varieties that are soft and sticky – though they need little tenderising, they can be added to the slow cooker at any stage during cooking.

Courgettes, cucumber, marrow and winter squash

Courgettes (zucchini): These are baby marrows and the younger they are picked, the more flavour they have. Slice or chop them and stir into soups, sauces, casseroles, rice dishes and so on. I prefer my courgettes to have some 'bite', so I add them to the slow cooker for only the final 30 minutes of cooking.

Cucumber: Halve lengthways, and scoop the seeds out and discard them. Chop or slice the flesh and stir it into rice or dishes containing grains just before serving.

Marrow (squash): The bland flavour and soft texture are particularly suitable for spicy casseroles made in the slow cooker. Peel, remove the seeds and chop the flesh into even-sized pieces before mixing with the other ingredients in the slow cooker.

Winter squash: The best-known varieties are butternut and acorn, but all squashes make particularly good soups and stews and are ideal in spicy dishes. When cooked, they have a lovely nutty flavour and a creamy texture. Remove the seeds, then peel the flesh and cut it into even-sized pieces before adding to the slow cooker.

Asparagus, celery and fennel

Asparagus: Best cooked for only a short time, asparagus can be cut into short lengths, then added to soups or casseroles during the final stages of cooking – for the last 1–2 hours.

Celery: This gives a wonderful flavour to slow-cooked soups, sauces and casseroles. Add it, chopped or sliced, with the onions and other vegetables at the start of cooking. I usually like to soften it first in a little oil or butter on the hob.

Fennel: This has a strong aniseed flavour that mellows with cooking to become mild and almost elusive. Trim and slice it, then add it to the slow cooker. Save any fronds from the top of the fennel bulb to chop and scatter over the cooked dish.

Beans, peas, sweetcorn, okra and beansprouts

Broad (fava), green and runner beans: Mix with the cooking liquid (and any other ingredients), bring just to the boil on the hob, then put into the slow cooker.

Peas, mangetout (snowpeas) and sugar snap peas: Add to the slow cooker for the final 30–40 minutes of cooking time. This way they will retain their freshness and their bite.

Sweetcorn (corn): Strip the kernels from the cob and add with the rest of the ingredients. Baby corn, though bland in flavour, adds crunch to a dish when sliced and stirred into a dish for about the last 30 minutes of cooking time.

Okra: Slice before adding to casseroles. It gives a glutinous consistency that serves to thicken the sauce and is particularly good in spicy dishes with strong flavours.

Beansprouts: These add an interesting texture to a casserole and are best added to the slow cooker for the final 30 minutes or so of cooking.

Pulses

Lentils: These need no pre-soaking. They may be added straight to the slow cooker.

Dried beans and peas: These must be soaked for several hours or overnight in plenty of cold water before slow cooking. This includes varieties such as borlotti, butter (lima), cannellini, flageolet and haricot (navy) beans, as well as whole green peas and chick peas (garbanzos).

Some dried beans, such as red kidney beans, must be boiled rapidly on the hob for 10 minutes (be guided by packet instructions). This is essential to destroy any toxins that could otherwise cause severe food poisoning. Once boiled, they can be drained and added to the slow cooker at the start of cooking.

To speed up cooking and to encourage dried beans and peas to cook evenly, I usually boil them for a short time before putting them in the slow cooker.

Canned pulses: These are ideal for the slow cooker. Though they are cooked already (which means you won't have to wait ages for them to tenderise), most varieties can happily stay in the slow cooker for several hours. Drain and rinse them well first. A 400 g/15 oz/large can is approximately equivalent to 100 g/4 oz dried uncooked.

Mushrooms

Fresh mushrooms give a mild, earthy flavour to many dishes in the slow cooker. For a delicate flavour and attractive appearance, use whole button mushrooms. Closed or open-cap mushrooms are good sliced and added to soups and rice dishes. Large flat mushrooms, chopped or sliced, add a dark colour and rich flavour to casseroles. My favourite all-purpose mushroom is the chestnut, which has a lovely brown colour, firm texture and nutty flavour.

Mushrooms that are added to the slow cooker early in the cooking process will impart most of their flavour to the dish. To appreciate the texture, and keep the flavour of milder varieties in particular, add them for the final 30 minutes.

Dried mushrooms: Varieties such as porcini, morels and ceps are widely available. These have an intense flavour. For the best of both worlds, mix them with fresh mushrooms to give a lovely balance of freshness and flavour. Soak the dried mushrooms in boiling water before use (check the packet instructions), then add to the slow cooker with the other ingredients at the start of cooking. The soaking water will be full of flavour and colour, so save it and add it to your recipe.

Canned mushrooms: These are best drained and added to the slow cooker 15–30 minutes before serving, stirring them gently into the other ingredients.

Brassicas and green leafy vegetables

This group includes broccoli, brussels sprouts, cabbage, cauliflower, chard, pak choi, sorrel, spinach and spring (collard) greens.

All these vegetables are ideal for casseroles and winter dishes. Some have quite strong flavours. Cut into small even-sized pieces or break into florets if appropriate. Cabbage and spinach are best thinly sliced, though baby spinach leaves can be stirred in whole. Add them to the other ingredients in the slow cooker towards the end of cooking, for the final 30 minutes to 1 hour.

Fresh herbs and salad leaves

I often like to add small whole or shredded salad leaves (such as Chinese leaf, lettuce, rocket, watercress) to a hot dish, until they are only just wilted. They should be stirred into the rest of the ingredients in the slow cooker just before serving. Fresh herbs may be added in the same way. Note that they are not really suitable for lengthy cooking.

STORECUPBOARD A–Z

I like to keep a supply of staple ingredients ready to hand so that I can put together a meal at a moment's notice. The list below is only a guide – you will want to customise it to suit your own requirements, adding your favourite ingredients.

Barley
This is most widely available as pearl barley, which is barley that has had its bran removed before being steamed and polished. It's delicious in soups and casseroles, helping them to thicken slightly.

For how to cook, see Barley in Pesto and Cream Sauce, page 57.

Buckwheat
Although this sounds as if it should be a grain, buckwheat is actually the triangular seed of a herb that is native to Russia. It can be bought plain or roasted, and cooked and served in similar ways to rice. It goes particularly well with full-flavoured root vegetables and garlic. Buckwheat groats are the hulled and crushed seeds of buckwheat.

To cook, add to a pan of water, according to the packet instructions, bring to the boil on the hob, transfer to the slow cooker and cook on High or Low until tender. Take care not to overcook it (you will need to check the cooking time in the manufacturer's instruction booklet to see what is right for your particular slow cooker).

Bulghar
Bulghar, also spelt bulgar or bulgur (cracked wheat), comprises wheat berries that have been steamed, dried and crushed. It is used frequently in Middle Eastern cuisine and its chewy texture makes it ideal for mixing with vegetables and for serving either hot or cold as a salad or as a side dish.

For how to cook, see Bulghar Wheat with Golden Onions, page 49.

Butter

When flavour is all-important, I like to use butter rather than any other fat in my recipes – in sponge puddings and cakes for example, for softening vegetables (particularly in soups) and for making garlic bread. Strict vegetarians can of course use a vegetarian alternative such as margarine or oil.

Coconut milk and cream

Coconut milk is available in cans and as a powder to be made up with water. Coconut cream is thicker than coconut milk and is usually available in small cartons. Creamed coconut is sold in blocks ready for chopping or grating straight into a dish to thicken it and also to add its sweet flavour.

Couscous

Couscous is made from grains of semolina (cream of wheat) and is a feature of North African cuisine. It needs only to be rehydrated so its 'cooking' time is short. Cook the main ingredients in the slow cooker in the usual way, then stir in the couscous 5–10 minutes before serving.

Dairy produce

Since my diet is not vegetarian, I like to have a stock of cream, yoghurt, crème fraîche and all types of cheese to use in my recipes. You can, of course, replace these with vegetarian alternatives such as soya milk, silken tofu and vegetarian cheese.

In general, dairy products are not suitable for long slow cooking – they tend to separate – and so are best added during the final 20–30 minutes of cooking.

See also Butter, above.

Dried fruit

Whole dried fruit is ideal for rehydrating in the slow cooker, and it makes a lovely dessert or breakfast dish. Dried fruit, such as apricots, raisins and golden raisins are also to be found in several other recipes in this book, savoury and sweet.

Eggs

You may not associate eggs with slow cooking, but it can be done. I find them useful for adding extra interest and nutritional value to a rice dish. About 15 minutes before serving, make indentations in the rice and crack an egg into each.

For hard-boiled (hard-cooked) eggs to accompany a dish, wrap them (individually) in foil and add to the slow cooker for the last 1–1½ hours.

Herbs

Dried herbs are better than fresh for long, slow cooking. I find dried thyme, oregano and mixed herbs most useful.

Fresh herbs, such as parsley, coriander (cilantro) and basil are best added near the end of cooking or just before serving.

Millet

This cereal grass can be cooked in similar ways to rice. Its taste is fairly bland, which makes it an ideal partner for spicy dishes and curries. To cook, add the millet to plenty of water, following the packet instructions, and bring to the boil, then transfer to the slow cooker and cook on High or Low until tender. Take care not to overcook it – the first time you cook it, watch it carefully and make a note of the cooking time in your particular slow cooker. Lightly toasting it before cooking adds a lovely nutty flavour.

Miso

This fermented bean paste can be made from barley, rice or soya beans and is a mainstay in Japanese dishes. It's available in a variety of flavours and colours and has a texture like peanut butter. A particular favourite of mine is an organic brown rice miso, which I have used in some of the recipes. Please feel free to use your own choice of miso in its place. I also keep some sachets of organic instant miso soup in my cupboard – another handy basis of a well-flavoured stock or sauce for any dish.

Mustard

There are three types in my cupboard – hot English for adding to dishes during the final few minutes of cooking, mild Dijon for stirring into a casserole just before serving, and wholegrain mustard for adding masses of flavour and 'bite' to dishes.

Nuts

Almonds, cashews, hazelnuts (filberts) and walnuts are my favourites and they can be used plain or toasted. Scatter them over finished dishes to add extra food value and a crunchy texture. Ground almonds are ideal in puddings and cakes and for thickening sauces. Chestnuts are available fresh, canned, vacuum-packed (my favourite) or dried, and add their own brand of floury sweetness to a recipe. Peanut butter is also handy for stirring into soups and casseroles for extra flavour (sometimes I add a spoonful of the smooth variety to the vegetable stock in a recipe).

Oats

Most people buy rolled oats, which have been crushed and can be used to make porridge. Whole oat grains (or groats) are also available and can be cooked and served like rice, as a side dish, salad or main dish with vegetables. They also make a deliciously creamy porridge.

For how to cook whole oats, see Whole Oat Porridge, page 58.

Oil

I generally have a bottle each of sunflower oil and light olive oil for cooking, plus extra-virgin olive oil for making dressings. Walnut and sesame oils are great for adding at the last minute to a cooked dish, to add their own particular flavour.

Olives

There are many different varieties – black, green, pitted and stuffed – and all are useful for adding flavour to casseroles. They should be added to the slow cooker just before serving or for the final 20–30 minutes of cooking.

Pasta

I like to keep a selection of pasta shapes, plus spaghetti. Whatever its shape and size, pasta is usually best added to the slow cooker for only the final 30–40 minutes of cooking – if you cook it for longer it will become mushy. Make sure there is sufficient liquid for the pasta to be immersed during cooking.

Polenta

Polenta (cornmeal) is a staple of Northern Italy. Stirred into soups and casseroles, it makes a useful thickening agent.

Pulses

Pulses – dried peas, beans and lentils – are excellent for long, slow cooking, and add flavour, texture and nutritional value to all sorts of dishes. I always keep a large selection of different types, both dried and canned. As you will see in my recipes, I tend to boil most dried beans and peas for a short time before putting them in the slow cooker – this softens them a little and encourages them to cook evenly. For full instructions on preparation of dried pulses, see pages 16–17. Canned pulses need no special preparation and require only a short cooking time.

Quinoa

This is an ancient South American grain that has recently experienced a revival in popularity. It is a high-protein grain that expands to four times its size during cooking. It has a delicate flavour and can be used in place of rice or couscous. Take care not to overcook quinoa – the first time you use it in the slow cooker, watch over it and check the cooking time carefully until you are used to it.

Quorn

Quorn is a mycoprotein derived from the mushroom family and is available minced (ground) and as pieces and steaks. It has a bland flavour and a texture that may be compared to that of chicken. It is usually sold frozen. It absorbs flavours readily and may be stirred into sauces, soups and casseroles in the slow cooker. Though it cooks quickly, I have found that it will sit quite happily, immersed in liquid in the slow cooker for several hours.

Rice

I most frequently use long-grain, basmati and brown rice. The cooking times are fairly short, even for brown rice, which takes longer than ordinary rice. For best results, I use the types labelled 'easy-cook'. These have been par-boiled and tend to be less starchy than ordinary varieties, so the grains are less likely to stick together. Always rinse rice thoroughly in cold water before cooking.

Apart from rice pudding, rice is not suitable for all-day cooking – and it is easy to overcook it in the slow cooker, so check the cooking time carefully in the manufacturer's instruction booklet for your particular model.

Seeds

Poppy, pumpkin, sesame and sunflower seeds add their own particular flavour and crunchy texture to a recipe, especially when lightly toasted. They also contain lots of protein, so they add nutritional value to vegetarian meals. I like to stir them into dishes made with rice, pasta and other grains.

Tahini is a thick paste made from ground sesame seeds and is particularly good stirred into soups and casseroles made with chick peas (garbanzos).

Sprouting seeds give a delicious crunchy texture to dishes. They are best added to a dish during the final 20–30 minutes of cooking.

Semolina

Semolina (cream of wheat) is coarsely ground durum wheat. It is useful in lots of cakes and puddings and I also like to sprinkle it into soups and casseroles, towards the end of cooking, as a thickening agent.

Soy sauce

There are two types. Light soy sauce is pale and tends to have a strong salty flavour, dark soy sauce adds colour and a sweet flavour. I use them both to add flavour to stock, soups, sauces and casseroles and to marinate tofu.

Spices

I like to keep a stock of whole and ground spices, such as cloves, cinnamon, ginger, nutmeg, turmeric, cumin, coriander, mixed (apple-pie) spice, etc. Add them to recipes in your slow cooker in the same way as when cooking conventionally.

Stock

To my mind, there is no substitute for homemade stock (see page 30), but I guess few of us have the time to make sufficient to cater for all our needs. However, there are some good stock products – cubes, concentrates, etc. – available in a wide variety of flavours to suit all recipes. My favourite is a vegetable bouillon powder that can either be made up with hot water or stirred straight into soups and casseroles. Sometimes I mix vegetable stock with a little miso or soy sauce for added flavour.

Whether using homemade or commercially produced stock, it is important not to use one with a flavour that is so pronounced that everything begins to taste the same.

Tofu

Tofu, or soya bean curd, is made from pressed curds of milk extracted from cooked soya beans. It is sold in blocks and is available in two forms, silken or firm. Silken tofu is light and creamy and is ideal for stirring into or topping dishes just before serving. Use it plain or flavoured with herbs and spices, in the same way you might use thick cream, yoghurt or crème fraîche. Firm tofu has been pressed for longer and can be cut into chunks that are ideal for frying (sautéing), grilling (broiling) and stirring into soups, sauces and casseroles. Firm tofu can be bought plain, marinated or smoked.

Plain tofu has a bland taste that readily absorbs flavours from other ingredients and can be marinated in ingredients such as soy sauce, sherry, oil, crushed ginger and garlic. Marinated tofu is ready prepared – usually marinated in soy sauce, yeast extract and seasonings. Smoked tofu is firm and has a flavour that is similar to mild smoked bacon.

Once a packet has been opened, any unused tofu should be stored in a container of cold water in the fridge for one or two days; the water should be changed daily (check the packet instructions for details).

Vinegar

I usually have red and white wine vinegar in the cupboard for adding to sauces and preserves. Rice vinegar is mild and slightly sweet and is ideal in oriental dishes. In addition, I like to keep balsamic condiment with its dark colour and rich, sweet flavour that is ideal for dressings and meals with an Italian flavour.

Wheat

Wheat grains, both whole and cracked or broken, can be cooked in the slow cooker and served hot or cold in salads, side dishes or main dishes. Following the packet instructions, bring the wheat and water to the boil on the hob, transfer to the slow cooker and cook on High or Low until tender. The first time you cook them, check the cooking time as this varies from one slow cooker to another. Whole, pre-cooked durum wheat grains are ideal for slow cooking too.

Wild rice

In fact, this is not rice but a grass. It has a distinctive, nutty flavour and a chewy texture. I like it best when mixed with other types of rice.

NOTES ON THE RECIPES

- All ingredients are given in metric, imperial and American measures. Follow one set only in a recipe. American terms are given in brackets.

- The ingredients are listed in the order in which they are used in the recipe.

- All spoon measures are level: 1 tsp = 5 ml; 1 tbsp = 15 ml.

- Eggs are medium unless otherwise stated. If you use a different size, adjust the amount of liquid you add to obtain the right consistency.

- Always wash, peel, core and seed, if necessary, fresh fruit and vegetables before use. Ensure that all produce is as fresh as possible and in good condition.

- Seasoning and the use of strongly flavoured ingredients, such as onions and garlic, are very much a matter of personal preference. Taste the food as you cook and adjust seasoning to suit.

- Always use fresh herbs unless dried are specifically called for. If it is necessary to use dried herbs, use half the quantity stated for fresh. Chopped frozen varieties are much better than dried. There is no substitute for fresh parsley and coriander (cilantro).

- Can and packet sizes are approximate and will vary according to the particular brand.

- I use butter in some of the recipes but you may prefer to substitute margarine or a spread of your choice. If using margarine, check that it is suitable for cooking.

- Use your own discretion in substituting ingredients and personalising the recipes. Make notes of particular successes as you go along.

- Use whichever kitchen gadgets you like to speed up preparation: a mixer for whisking, food processor for grating, slicing, mixing or kneading, blender for liquidising, etc.

- Some recipes use dairy products. Vegans should either omit them or use vegan alternatives such as soya milk products. Cheeses, margarine and yoghurt that are suitable for strict vegetarians are usually clearly marked on the labels.

- Some recipes use processed foods, such as canned vegetables, biscuits (cookies) and ready-made seasonings and condiments. Check the product labels to be certain of their suitability for vegetarians.

- It is worth nothing that some alcoholic drinks use animal-derived products in their production.

SOUPS

Soups and slow cooking go hand in hand. The long cooking time ensures that all those delicious flavours have time to mingle gently and develop, creating the most delicious and nutritious results.

The basis of any good soup is a well-flavoured stock, so the first recipe in this section is for home-made vegetable stock. If you are short of time, however, you can use a good-quality stock cube or powder or ready-made chilled stock from your supermarket.

Soups are wonderfully versatile. Served on their own, they make a perfect starter for any kind of meal, but you will also find recipes in this section that are hearty enough to serve as a complete meal in themselves, teamed with a chunk of fresh crusty bread or a sandwich.

I often make vegetable stock with odds and ends of vegetables lurking in the fridge. You can use fennel, parsnip and mushrooms as well as those used in this recipe. Just throw everything into the slow cooker and several hours later you will have a light and flavourful stock.

slow-cooked
vegetable stock

SERVES 4–6

2 onions, chopped
2 carrots, skins left on and chopped
2 celery sticks, chopped
1 large baking potato, skin left on and
  thickly sliced

At least 4 whole garlic cloves
2 bay leaves
A few sprigs of fresh parsley
2.5 ml/½ tsp whole black peppercorns
2.5 ml/½ tsp salt (optional)

1 Put all the ingredients into the slow cooker and pour over sufficient boiling water to cover them.

2 Cover and cook on Low for 8–10 hours or on High for 3–4 hours until all the vegetables are tender.

3 Strain and use the same day. Alternatively, cool completely and freeze until required.

If you use fresh chestnuts, they will need part-cooking and peeling first. Make a slit in the outer skin of each, put them in a pan of cold water, bring to the boil and boil for about 5 minutes. Lift them out, a few at a time, and peel off both the tough outer and thin inner skins.

chestnut soup with vegetables and orange

SERVES 4–6

25 g/1 oz/2 tbsp butter or margarine
1 large onion, finely chopped
1 carrot, finely chopped
100 g/4 oz mushrooms, sliced
7.5 ml/1½ tsp plain (all-purpose) flour
1 litre/1¾ pts/4¼ cups vegetable stock

240 g/9 oz/small can of peeled chestnuts
Salt and freshly ground black pepper
10 ml/2 tsp finely grated orange zest
Chopped fresh parsley, to garnish

1 Preheat the slow cooker on High.

2 Melt the butter or margarine in a large pan, add the onion, carrot and mushrooms and cook, stirring occasionally, until softened and just beginning to brown.

3 Add the flour and cook, stirring, for a few minutes until the ingredients are lightly browned.

4 Remove from the heat and gradually stir in the stock. Add the chestnuts and seasoning.

5 Bring just to the boil, stirring. Transfer to the slow cooker and stir gently.

6 Cover and cook on Low for 6–8 hours until all the ingredients are soft and cooked through.

7 Purée the soup until fairly smooth, then stir in the orange zest.

8 Reheat in the slow cooker on High for about 20 minutes or in a pan on the hob. Adjust the seasoning before serving if you wish, and garnish with parsley.

This soup can also be made with two large cans of drained beans, in which case you should start at Step 3 and add the beans with the garlic and tomatoes at Step 4. The cooked soup is ladled over slices of rustic Italian bread and finished with a drizzle of olive oil.

thick traditional
tuscan bean soup

SERVES 4–6

225 g/8 oz dried cannellini or borlotti beans, soaked overnight in plenty of cold water
15 ml/1 tbsp olive oil, plus extra to serve
1 large onion, cut into small dice
2 carrots, cut into small dice
2 leeks, thinly sliced
2 celery sticks, thinly sliced
2 garlic cloves, finely chopped
8 oz/225 g/small can of chopped tomatoes
900 ml/1½ pts/3¾ cups vegetable stock
Salt and freshly ground black pepper
1 courgette (zucchini), cut into very small dice
A handful of baby spinach leaves
30 ml/2 tbsp green pesto
4 thick slices of Italian bread, such as ciabatta

1 Preheat the slow cooker on High.

2 Drain the beans, put into a large pan and cover with cold water. Bring to the boil and boil gently for 10 minutes.

3 Meanwhile, heat the oil in a large pan and add the onion, carrots, leeks and celery. Cook over a medium heat, stirring frequently, until just beginning to brown.

4 Drain the beans and add to the pan with the garlic, tomatoes, stock and a little seasoning. Bring just to the boil, then transfer to the slow cooker and stir gently.

5 Cover and cook on Low for 6–8 hours or until the vegetables are very tender, then stir in the courgette and spinach and cook for a further 30 minutes until soft.

6 Toast the bread until golden brown.

7 Stir the pesto into the soup, then ladle the soup into bowls.

8 Top each with hot toasted bread and drizzle with olive oil.

This thick soup is simplicity itself to make and is hearty enough to serve as a main dish when accompanied with lots of warm crusty bread. It is comfort food at its best, and would be wonderfully welcoming to come home to in winter after a stressful day at work.

thick mixed vegetable chowder

SERVES 4–6

25 g/1 oz/2 tbsp butter or margarine
1 large onion, finely chopped
4 celery sticks, thinly sliced
1 potato, cut into small dice
1 carrot, thinly sliced
1 small celeriac (celery root), cut into cubes
100 g/4 oz green beans, halved crossways

1 litre/1¾ pts/4¼ cups vegetable stock
1 small green (bell) pepper, finely chopped
150 ml/¼ pt/⅔ cup double (heavy) cream
175 g/6 oz drained canned sweetcorn
Salt and freshly ground black pepper
Chopped fresh dill or parsley, to garnish

1 Preheat the slow cooker on High.

2 Melt the butter or margarine in a large pan, add the onion, celery, potato and carrot and cook, stirring occasionally, until softened but not browned.

3 Add the celeriac, beans and stock and bring just to the boil. Transfer to the slow cooker and stir gently.

4 Cover and cook on Low for 6–8 hours or until tender. Stir in the green pepper, cream and sweetcorn and cook for a further 30 minutes.

5 Adjust the seasoning and serve garnished with dill or parsley.

This soup needs hardly any preparation at all. It is made using ingredients that you will probably have to hand at any time and the simple vegetables work well with the addition of wholegrain mustard to make a nutritious complete lunch or light supper.

vegetable soup with cheese and wholegrain mustard

SERVES 4

15 ml/1 tbsp olive oil
1 large onion, finely chopped
4 carrots, thinly sliced
2 celery sticks, thinly sliced
1 small potato, cut into small dice
450 ml/¾ pt/2 cups vegetable stock

30 ml/2 tbsp plain (all-purpose) flour
300 ml/½ pt/1¼ cups milk
15 ml/1 tbsp wholegrain mustard
100 g/4 oz/1 cup grated hard cheese, such as Cheddar
Salt and freshly ground black pepper

1 Preheat the slow cooker on High.

2 Heat the oil in a large pan, add the onion, carrots, celery and potato. Cook, stirring occasionally, until slightly softened but not quite browned.

3 Add the stock and bring just to the boil. Transfer to the slow cooker and stir gently.

4 Cover and cook on Low for 6–8 hours until all the ingredients are soft and cooked through.

5 Blend the flour with a little of the milk to make a smooth paste. Stir the paste into the hot soup with the remaining milk and the mustard and cook for a further 30–40 minutes.

6 Just before serving, stir in half the cheese until melted. Adjust the seasoning to taste.

7 Ladle the soup into warm bowls and serve sprinkled with the remaining cheese.

*The wonderful fragrance and sweet, delicate flavour of fennel matches
well with the cannellini beans. Save some of the feathery fronds from the
top of the fennel bulb for garnishing. Blending only half the soup and
leaving the rest chunky gives the soup an appealing texture.*

white bean and fennel soup
with blue cheese

SERVES 4–6

30 ml/2 tbsp olive oil
1 onion, finely chopped
1 leek, thinly sliced
2 garlic cloves, crushed
1 fennel bulb, thinly sliced
900 ml/1½ pts/3¾ cups
    vegetable stock

425 g/15 oz/large can of cannellini
    beans, drained
300 ml/½ pt/1¼ cups milk
Salt and freshly ground pepper
15 ml/1 tbsp lemon juice
50 g/2 oz/½ cup crumbled blue
    cheese, such as Stilton

1 Preheat the slow cooker on High.

2 Heat the oil in a large pan, add the onion, leek, garlic and fennel.
Cook gently, stirring occasionally, until softened and just
beginning to brown.

3 Add the stock and beans and bring just to the boil. Transfer to the
slow cooker and stir gently.

4 Cover and cook on Low for 6–8 hours until all the ingredients are
very tender.

5 Purée half the soup just until it is thick and chunky. Return to the
slow cooker, stir in the milk and adjust the seasoning to taste.

6 Cover and cook on High for 15–20 minutes until reheated.

7 Just before serving, stir in the lemon juice.

8 Ladle the soup into warm bowls and serve topped with crumbled
blue cheese.

The onions are first browned in a pan, then cooked gently in the slow cooker until they are meltingly soft, with a lovely rich flavour. I have suggested using Gruyère cheese on the bread, but just about any grated hard cheese of your choice, such as Cheddar, should work.

caramelised red onion soup with thyme

SERVES 4

30 ml/2 tbsp olive oil
4 large red onions, cut into thin
   wedges
5 ml/1 tsp sugar
1 large garlic clove, finely chopped
2.5 ml/½ tsp dried herbes de
   Provence or thyme

900 ml/1½ pts/3¾ cups vegetable
   stock
Salt and freshly ground black pepper
4 slices of French bread
100 g/4 oz/1 cup grated Gruyère
   (Swiss) cheese

1 Preheat the slow cooker on High.

2 Heat the oil in a large, shallow pan, add the onions and sugar and cook, stirring occasionally, until softened and browned all over.

3 Stir in the garlic, herbs or thyme, stock and seasoning and bring to the boil. Transfer to the slow cooker and stir gently.

4 Cover and cook on Low for 6–8 hours until all the ingredients are very tender.

5 When ready to serve, top the slices of bread with cheese, grill (broil) until bubbling and golden brown. Ladle the soup into warm bowls, then float one piece of bread on top of each serving of soup. Alternatively, ladle the soup into flameproof serving dishes, top with the cheese-topped bread and put under a hot grill (broiler) until bubbling and golden brown.

This recipe uses one of those wonderfully convenient packets of ready-prepared stir-fry vegetables, though if you have the time you could, of course, prepare your own selection of vegetables. The brown rice miso is not essential, but it does add a lovely flavour.

oriental vegetable soup with pan-fried tofu

SERVES 4

500 g/18 oz packet of prepared stir-fry vegetables
6 spring onions (scallions)
1 litre/1¾ pts/4¼ cups vegetable stock
30 ml/2 tbsp soy sauce

15 ml/1 tbsp tomato purée (paste)
10 ml/2 tsp brown rice miso
5 ml/1 tsp sugar
250 g/9 oz packet of firm tofu, drained and cut into cubes
15 ml/1 tbsp olive oil

1 Preheat the slow cooker on High.

2 Put the stir-fry vegetables into a large pan. Thinly slice the white parts of the spring onions and add to the pan, reserving the green parts for later. Add the stock, 15 ml/1 tbsp of the soy sauce, the tomato purée, miso and sugar.

3 Bring just to the boil, transfer to the slow cooker and stir gently.

4 Cover and cook on High for 2½–3½ hours until all the ingredients are tender.

5 Meanwhile, sprinkle the remaining soy sauce over the tofu, cover and leave to stand.

6 Just before serving, heat the oil in a frying pan (skillet), add the tofu and cook quickly until golden brown on all sides.

7 Stir the tofu and the reserved green onion tops into the soup.

8 Ladle into warm bowls and serve.

*This is a no-hassle dish that can be rustled up from storecupboard
ingredients in next to no time. Instead of canned tomatoes, you could use
the same weight of cherry tomatoes and add them at the end of Step 2
before stirring in the rest of the ingredients so they soften a little.*

butter bean, tomato and artichoke soup

SERVES 4–6

30 ml/2 tbsp olive oil
1 onion, finely chopped
1 garlic clove, finely chopped
400 g/14 oz/large can of chopped
   tomatoes
425 g/15 oz/large can of butter (lima)
   beans, drained

425 g/15 oz/large can of artichoke
   hearts, drained and halved
5 ml/1 tsp dried thyme
900 ml/1½ pts/3¾ cups vegetable
   stock
Salt and freshly ground black pepper
Chopped fresh herbs, such as
   parsley, fennel or basil, to garnish

1   Preheat the slow cooker on High.

2   Heat the oil in a large pan, add the onion and garlic and cook,
stirring occasionally, until slightly softened but not browned.

3   Stir in all the remaining ingredients.

4   Bring just to the boil, transfer to the slow cooker and stir gently.

5   Cover and cook on Low for 6–10 hours until all of the ingredients
are tender.

6   Adjust the seasoning to taste, then ladle into warm bowls and
serve sprinkled with herbs.

This filling soup is a great starter or light lunch, but it could equally well be served as a main dish if you added more cheese. The finished soup is attractively coloured thanks to the spinach and green pesto and the grated lemon zest adds a little extra something to the flavour.

celeriac, rice and spinach soup with pesto

SERVES 4–6

30 ml/2 tbsp olive oil
1 onion, finely chopped
350 g/12 oz celeriac (celery root), cut into dice
2.5 ml/½ tsp dried oregano
10 ml/2 tsp ground coriander
50 g/2 oz/¼ cup easy-cook long-grain rice
1.2 litres/2 pts/5 cups vegetable stock

Finely grated zest of ½ lemon
Salt and freshly ground black pepper
15 ml/1 tbsp green pesto
2 large handfuls of baby spinach leaves
50 g/2 oz/½ cup shavings of Parmesan cheese, to garnish

1 Preheat the slow cooker on High.

2 Heat the oil in a large pan, add the onion and cook, stirring occasionally, until very soft but not browned.

3 Stir in the celeriac, oregano, coriander and rice.

4 Add the stock and lemon zest.

5 Bring just to the boil, transfer to the slow cooker and stir gently.

6 Cover and cook on High for 1½–2½ hours until the vegetables are soft and the rice is completely cooked.

7 Taste and adjust the seasoning.

8 Just before serving, add the pesto and the spinach and stir until the leaves wilt.

9 Serve in warm bowls, garnished with Parmesan cheese.

Minestrone is a classic soup and just about every Italian household will have its own version – though it just wouldn't be a minestrone without tomatoes, beans and pasta. It is a healthy and satisfying soup, delicious topped with a sprinkling of Parmesan cheese.

traditional italian minestrone

SERVES 4–6

30 ml/2 tbsp olive oil
1 onion, finely chopped
1 large garlic clove, finely chopped
2 carrots, cut into small dice
2 celery sticks, thinly sliced
900 ml/1½ pts/3¾ cups vegetable stock
4 sun-dried tomatoes, finely chopped

300 g/11 oz/1 medium can of haricot (navy) beans, drained
Salt and freshly ground black pepper
A handful of small pasta shapes
A large handful of finely shredded cabbage
45 ml/3 tbsp chopped fresh parsley

1   Preheat the slow cooker on High.

2   Heat the oil in a large pan and add the onion, garlic, carrots and celery. Cook, stirring occasionally, until slightly softened.

3   Stir in the stock, tomatoes, beans and seasoning.

4   Bring to the boil, transfer to the slow cooker and stir gently.

5   Cover and cook on Low for 6–8 hours or until all the vegetables are tender. Add the pasta and cabbage and cook for a further 30 minutes until the cabbage is soft and the pasta cooked through.

6   Just before serving, adjust the seasoning to taste and stir in the parsley. Serve in warm bowls.

This nutritious soup can also be made without the tofu. Instead, top some thick slices of rustic bread with wholegrain mustard and grated cheese and place under a preheated grill until the cheese is bubbling and golden. Float the slices on top of the soup just before serving.

green lentil soup with tofu

SERVES 4–6

30 ml/2 tbsp olive oil
1 onion, thinly sliced
1 garlic clove, finely chopped
150 g/5 oz/generous ⅔ cup green
   lentils
1 litre/1¾ pts/4¼ cups vegetable
   stock

15 ml/1 tbsp mushroom ketchup
   (catsup)
5 ml/1 tsp dried thyme
10 ml/2 tsp balsamic condiment
Salt and freshly ground black pepper
50 g/2 oz/½ cup silken tofu, blended
   until smooth
30 ml/2 tbsp green pesto

1 Preheat the slow cooker on High.

2 Heat the oil in a large pan, add the onion and garlic and cook, stirring occasionally, until slightly softened but not browned.

3 Stir in the lentils, stock, mushroom ketchup and thyme.

4 Bring to the boil, transfer to the slow cooker and stir gently.

5 Cover and cook on Low for 8–10 hours until all the ingredients are soft.

6 Just before serving, stir in the balsamic condiment and season to taste with salt and pepper.

7 Ladle into warm bowls and top each serving with a large spoonful of tofu and a drizzle of pesto.

STARTERS, SIDE DISHES AND LIGHT MEALS

As I put together each of the recipes in this section, I found myself wondering, 'Is this a dish to start a meal, or is it suitable as an accompaniment? Or is it really a snack?' The answer, as I soon realised, is that many of them are suitable to be all three. While the choice is yours, I have included what I hope are helpful serving suggestions in the introduction to each recipe.

This recipe is so versatile – a great accompaniment to curries and other spiced dishes, but also good served cold as part of a buffet. It makes a good side dish for a barbecue too; because it is slow cooked you won't have to keep running between kitchen and garden to check on it!

aromatic rice
with ginger and chillies

SERVES 4

15 ml/1 tbsp olive oil
25 g/1 oz/2 tbsp butter or margarine
5 ml/1 tsp mustard seeds
6 curry leaves
2.5 cm/1 in piece of fresh root ginger, peeled and very finely chopped

2 garlic cloves, very thinly sliced
5 ml/1 tsp salt
350 g/12 oz/1½ cups easy-cook basmati rice
4 small red or green chillies, or a mixture of both

1 Preheat the slow cooker on High.

2 Heat the oil and butter or margarine in a pan, add the mustard seeds, curry leaves, ginger, garlic and salt. Cook, stirring, for about 2 minutes without browning.

3 Add the rice and whole chillies and cook, stirring, for 1 minute.

4 Stir in 750 ml/1¼ pts/3 cups of water and bring just to the boil. Transfer to the slow cooker and stir gently.

5 Cover and cook on High for 1 hour, then stir gently. Replace the lid and continue to cook for 30 minutes to 1 hour, until all the liquid has been absorbed and everything is tender.

6 Serve immediately.

This is a delicious, aromatic accompaniment to vegetarian dishes. If you don't have fresh mint, use 5 ml/1 tsp of dried mint and add it with the stock. To make this a main meal, serve it topped with thinly sliced red onion, cubes of Mozzarella cheese and a few black olives.

vegetable couscous with lemon and mint

SERVES 4–6

45 ml/3 tbsp olive oil
2 leeks, thinly sliced
1 carrot, thinly sliced
1 celery stick, thinly sliced
1 garlic clove, finely chopped
600 ml/1 pt/2 cups vegetable stock

225 g/8 oz/1½ cups couscous
Finely grated zest of 1 lemon
Juice of ½ lemon
100 g/4 oz cherry tomatoes, halved
1–2 tbsp/15–30 ml finely chopped
   fresh mint

1   Preheat the slow cooker on High.

2   Heat 15 ml/1 tbsp of the oil in a pan, add the leeks, carrot, celery and garlic and cook, stirring occasionally, until softened but not browned.

3   Add the stock, bring just to the boil and transfer to the slow cooker.

4   Cover and cook on Low for 5–8 hours until all the vegetables are tender.

5   Stir in the remaining ingredients, cover and cook for a further 5–10 minutes until the liquid has been absorbed and the couscous is fluffy.

6   Gently stir in the remaining oil and serve immediately.

Which squash you buy will depend on the shape and size of your slow cooker. For a change, instead of serving the squash whole, scoop the cooked flesh out of the skin, mash it with the sauce and serve it topped with buttered crumbs or croûtons.

butternut squash with fragrant ginger and coriander sauce

SERVES 2

1 acorn or small butternut squash
600 ml/1 pt/2 cups vegetable stock
2.5 ml/½ tsp ground cumin
4 cm/1½ in piece of fresh root ginger

45 ml/3 tbsp double (heavy) cream
30 ml/2 tbsp chopped fresh coriander
(cilantro)

1 Halve the squash lengthways and scoop out the seeds.

2 Pour the stock into the slow cooker and stir in the cumin.

3 Roughly grate the ginger, skin and all. Gather the gratings in one hand and, holding them over the slow cooker, squeeze tightly so that the juice runs through your fingers into the stock. Once every last drop has been squeezed out, discard the gratings.

4 Lay the squash, cut side down, in the liquid.

5 Cover and cook on Low for 4–5 hours until the squash is very tender.

6 Carefully transfer the squash to a serving dish and keep warm.

7 Tip the juices into a shallow pan, bring to the boil and bubble until reduced to about 75 ml/5 tbsp. Add the cream and bubble for 1 minute. Stir in the coriander.

8 Serve the squash with the sauce spooned into the cavities.

This makes a very tasty side dish but it is also ideal as a starter if you serve it with chunks of fresh crusty bread. As a change from Parmesan cheese, try using slices of Mozzarella instead, grilled until melted. If possible, choose short, fat fennel bulbs.

fennel with tomatoes, lemon and parmesan

SERVES 4

2 large fennel bulbs
30 ml/2 tbsp olive oil
400 g/14 oz/large can of chopped
    tomatoes
Salt and freshly ground black pepper

Finely grated zest and juice
    of ½ lemon
10 ml/2 tsp sugar
150 ml/¼ pt/⅔ cup vegetable stock
60 ml/4 tbsp freshly grated Parmesan
    cheese

1   Trim the fennel and cut lengthways into quarters, leaving the base intact and reserving any fronds from the tops.

2   Heat the oil in a frying pan (skillet), add the fennel and cook over a high heat until golden brown on all sides. Lift out and arrange in the slow cooker in an even layer.

3   To the pan, add the tomatoes, seasoning, lemon zest and juice, sugar and stock. Bring just to the boil and pour over the fennel.

4   Cover and cook on High for 5–8 hours until soft and tender.

5   Carefully spoon the fennel and sauce into a shallow flameproof dish.

6   Sprinkle with the Parmesan and put under a hot grill (broiler) until bubbling and golden brown.

*This is a wonderfully versatile recipe you will want to make again
and again. You can serve it hot or at room temperature, spooned
onto a bed of crisp salad leaves, as a perfect starter or light lunch. I also
like it with a plain or herb-filled omelette to make a satisfying supper.*

beans with oregano and balsamic dressing

SERVES 4–6

225 g/8 oz/1¼ cups dried beans,
   such as haricot (navy), borlotti or
   red kidney, soaked overnight in
   plenty of cold water
2 bay leaves
15 ml/1 tbsp dried oregano
60 ml/4 tbsp olive oil

15 ml/1 tbsp balsamic condiment
Salt and freshly ground black pepper
1–2 tbsp/15–30 ml fresh oregano
   leaves
A few thinly sliced red onion rings,
   to garnish

1 Preheat the slow cooker on High.

2 Drain the beans, put into a large pan and cover with cold water.
Bring to the boil and boil rapidly for 10 minutes.

3 Drain the beans and put into the slow cooker with the bay leaves
and dried oregano. Stir in 2 litres/3½ pts/8½ cups of boiling water.

4 Cover and cook on High for 8–12 hours until the beans are tender.

5 Drain the beans, discarding the liquid.

6 Combine the remaining ingredients and pour over the hot beans,
stirring gently.

7 Scatter the red onion rings over before serving.

The combination of fragrant spices in this dhal makes it delicious enough to eat on its own with naans or other Indian breads to mop it up. But it is also good served with basmati rice, mango chutney and raita, or a selection of curries or vegetable kebabs.

lentil dhal with onion, garlic and cumin

SERVES 4–6

250 g/9 oz/1½ cups split red lentils
2.5 cm/1 in piece of fresh root ginger, peeled and grated
5 ml/1 tsp ground coriander (cilantro)
1.5 ml/¼ tsp ground turmeric

1.5 ml/¼ tsp chilli powder
60 ml/4 tbsp olive oil
1 small onion, thinly sliced
2 garlic cloves, thinly sliced
5 ml/1 tsp cumin seeds

1   Preheat the slow cooker on High.

2   Put the lentils into the slow cooker with the ginger, coriander, turmeric and chilli powder. Pour in 900 ml/1½ pts/3¾ cups of boiling water and stir.

3   Cover and cook on Low for 8–10 hours or until tender. Stir once or twice after 4–5 hours if possible.

4   Heat the oil in a frying pan (skillet), add the onion, garlic and cumin seeds and cook quickly, stirring frequently, until crisp and brown.

5   Drizzle the onion mixture over the dhal and serve immediately.

Though the miso is optional, it does give the bulghar a wonderful flavour. Serve the dish hot as an accompaniment to savoury tarts or vegetarian sausages. Or serve cold as a starter or light lunch, with chopped tomato, cucumber and celery and crumbled Lancashire or Feta cheese stirred in.

bulghar wheat with golden onions

SERVES 4–6

25 g/1 oz/2 tbsp butter or margarine
1 onion, thinly sliced
175 g/6 oz/1½ cups bulghar (cracked wheat)

450 ml/¾ pt/2 cups vegetable stock
5 ml/1 tsp brown rice miso (optional)

1 Preheat the slow cooker on High.

2 Melt the butter or margarine in a pan, add the onion and cook gently, stirring occasionally, until softened and golden brown.

3 Put the bulghar into the slow cooker.

4 Stir the stock and miso (if using) into the onion and bring just to the boil.

5 Pour the onion mixture over the bulghar and stir gently.

6 Cover and cook on High for 1 hour until all the liquid has been absorbed.

7 Fluff up with a fork before serving.

A very pretty dish that takes its attractive colour and subtle flavour from the delicious saffron. Serve it as an elegant starter or light meal just as it is, or as an accompaniment to grilled goats' cheese, quiche, stir-fried vegetables or delicately flavoured casseroles.

basmati rice with saffron, broad beans and herbs

SERVES 4–6

A pinch of saffron strands
40 g/1½ oz/3 tbsp butter or
  margarine
225 g/8 oz leeks, thinly sliced
200 g/7 oz/generous ¾ cup easy-
  cook basmati rice

Salt
300 g/11 oz/medium can of broad
  (lima) beans, drained
30 ml/2 tbsp chopped fresh parsley
30 ml/2 tbsp chopped fresh coriander
  (cilantro)

1 Put the saffron into a measuring jug and pour over 600 ml/ 1 pt/2½ cups of boiling water. Leave to stand for 10 minutes.

2 Preheat the slow cooker on High.

3 Melt the butter or margarine in a pan, add the leeks and cook, stirring occasionally, until softened but not browned.

4 Stir in the rice and season with salt.

5 Add the saffron liquid and bring just to the boil. Transfer to the slow cooker and stir gently.

6 Cover and cook on High for 1–2 hours, stirring gently after 45 minutes, until almost all the liquid has been absorbed.

7 Stir in the beans and herbs, cover and leave to stand for 5–10 minutes. Fluff up with a fork and serve.

This is delicious served as an accompaniment to spiced dishes that have plenty of sauce to mop up. Remember that ordinary rice won't be very successful in a slow cooker so you should buy basmati rice labelled 'easy-cook' – and the rice must be rinsed well before adding to the crock pot.

coconut rice with garlic and coriander

SERVES 4–6

30 ml/2 tbsp olive oil
1 onion, finely chopped
1 garlic clove, finely chopped
200 g/7 oz/generous ¾ cup easy-
    cook basmati rice

90 ml/6 tbsp desiccated (shredded)
    coconut
Salt
Chopped fresh coriander (cilantro),
    to garnish

1 Preheat the slow cooker on High.

2 Heat the oil in a pan, add the onion and garlic and cook, stirring occasionally, until softened but not browned.

3 Stir in the rice, coconut and 750 ml/1¼ pts/3 cups of water.

4 Season with salt and bring just to the boil. Transfer to the slow cooker and stir gently.

5 Cover and cook on High for 1–1½ hours, stirring gently after 1 hour, until all the liquid has been absorbed.

6 Serve immediately, sprinkled with coriander.

This colourful Italian recipe needs little preparation and only needs a quick stir part way through cooking. Serve it as a starter or as an accompaniment to rice- or pasta-based dishes. To add protein and make this a lovely main dish, top it with stir-fried tofu.

italian-style peperonata

SERVES 6

60 ml/4 tbsp olive oil
2 onions, thinly sliced
2 garlic cloves, finely chopped
2 red (bell) peppers, cut into 2.5 cm/ 1 in wide strips

2 yellow peppers, cut into 2.5 cm/1 in wide strips
400 g/14 oz/large can of chopped tomatoes
Salt and freshly ground pepper

1 Preheat the slow cooker on High.

2 Heat the oil in a large pan, add the onions and garlic and cook, stirring occasionally, until softened and lightly browned.

3 Add the peppers, then stir in the tomatoes and seasoning.

4 Bring to the boil and transfer to the slow cooker, pressing down the peppers and levelling the surface.

5 Cover and cook on Low for 7–10 hours until the peppers are very soft. Stir once or twice if possible after 5 hours.

6 Taste and adjust the seasoning before serving.

Buckwheat has a lovely nutty flavour – and it's actually a herb,
not a grain as many people think. It cooks quickly, so be careful to keep
to the time I specify. Serve it as a starter or light meal or to accompany
grilled tomatoes, roasted vegetables or vegetables baked with cheese.

buckwheat with onion and sugar snap peas

SERVES 4–6

30 ml/2 tbsp olive oil
1 large onion, thinly sliced
175 g/6 oz/1 cup buckwheat
600 ml/1 pt/2½ cups vegetable stock
A handful of sugar snap peas

Salt and freshly ground black pepper
15–30 ml/2–3 tbsp chopped fresh
  parsley
25 g/1 oz/2 tbsp butter or margarine

1 Heat the oil in a large pan, add the onion and cook, stirring occasionally, until very soft and golden brown.

2 Stir in the buckwheat. Add the stock, bring just to the boil and transfer to the slow cooker. Scatter the sugar snap peas on top.

3 Cover and cook on High for about 1–1½ hours, stirring gently after 1 hour, until tender.

4 Fluff up the buckwheat with a fork, add seasoning to taste and stir in the parsley and butter or margarine.

5 Serve immediately.

The flavour explosion as the spice seeds burst in your mouth is sensational. I like to serve this dish before a curry, to tempt the appetite and excite the taste buds for the spices to follow. It's also good served with eggs, cooked in just about any way you like.

baby potatoes with whole spices and a cream sauce

SERVES 4

30 ml/2 tbsp olive oil
5 ml/1 tsp mustard seeds
5 ml/1 tsp fennel seeds
5 ml/1 tsp cumin seeds
2.5 ml/½ tsp coriander seeds
750 g/1¾ lb baby potatoes, halved

Salt and freshly ground black pepper
150 ml/¼ pt/⅔ cup vegetable stock
45 ml/3 tbsp double (heavy) cream
15 ml/1 tbsp chopped fresh parsley
15 ml/1 tbsp chopped fresh mint

1 Preheat the slow cooker on High.

2 Heat the oil in a frying pan (skillet), add the seeds and cook, stirring. As soon as they begin to pop and jump, add the potatoes and toss until well coated with the oil and seeds. Cook quickly, stirring frequently, until the potatoes are beginning to brown.

3 Transfer to the slow cooker, season with salt and pepper and pour the stock over.

4 Cover and cook on High for 1 hour or until the potatoes are tender.

5 Stir in the cream, cover and cook for 5 minutes.

6 Stir in the herbs and serve.

Even if you're not cooking for 8–10 people, it's worth making the large quantity I give here because any that doesn't get eaten on the day will freeze so well and will just need reheating. It makes an excellent side dish served with hearty vegetarian burgers, sausages, pies and casseroles.

slow-cooked red cabbage with apple

SERVES 8–10

1 small red cabbage, about 700 g/ 1½ lb, thinly sliced
2 onions, thinly sliced
1 large eating (dessert) apple, grated with the peel

150 ml/¼ pt/⅔ cup vegetable stock
30 ml/2 tbsp red wine vinegar
15 ml/1 tbsp sugar
Salt and freshly ground black pepper
50 g/2 oz/¼ cup butter or margarine

1 In a large bowl, combine all the ingredients except the butter or margarine and mix well.

2 Transfer to the slow cooker, packing the mixture down firmly.

3 Cover and cook on Low for 6–8 hours, stirring once or twice during the final 1–2 hours. All the ingredients should be very soft.

4 Cut the butter or margarine in pieces and stir into the cabbage, adjusting the seasoning to taste.

5 Serve hot or at room temperature.

These meltingly soft and luscious onions are so easy to prepare!
They make a delicious accompaniment to cheesy baked vegetables and
stir-fried tofu, a pizza topping along with black olives and cheese, as a tart
filling, or stirred into rice or couscous.

slow-cooked
caramelised onions

SERVES UP TO 8

4 onions, about 900 g/2 lb, thinly
   sliced
60 ml/4 tbsp olive oil

15 ml/1 tbsp sugar
5 ml/1 tsp cumin seeds
Salt and freshly ground black pepper

1 Put the sliced onions into the slow cooker.

2 Drizzle the oil over and toss the onions until evenly coated.

3 Stir in the sugar and cumin seeds.

4 Level the surface, pressing the onions down so they are well packed.

5 Cover and cook on Low for 10–12 hours, stirring occasionally after the first 4 hours. The onions should be meltingly soft and pale golden brown.

6 Season to taste with salt and pepper before serving.

I just love the velvety texture of pearl barley, particularly when served in this simple way. It makes a perfect accompaniment to pies and tarts, grilled mushrooms or roasted vegetables. It also makes a lovely light meal with a crisp green salad.

barley in pesto and cream sauce

SERVES 4

225 g/8 oz/generous 1 cup pearl barley
3 tbsp/45 ml double (heavy) cream
3 tbsp/45 ml green pesto

Salt and freshly ground black pepper
50 g/2 oz/½ cup shavings of Parmesan cheese (optional)

1 Put the barley into the slow cooker and stir in 1 litre/1¾ pts/ 4¼ cups of boiling water.

2 Cover and cook on High for 1½–2 hours until the barley is just tender.

3 Drain and return the barley to the slow cooker.

4 Stir the cream into the pesto, pour over the barley and mix well. Season to taste with salt and pepper.

5 Serve immediately, topped with shavings of Parmesan, if using.

Whole oat grain is ideal for slow cooking porridge overnight. It will have a lovely texture and nutty flavour. I like it with a light sprinkling of sugar and ice-cold milk poured over the top – just spoon the hot porridge through the cold milk and enjoy! For a richer flavour, try it with cream.

slow-cooked
whole oat porridge

SERVES 4–6

125 g/4½ oz/generous ½ cup whole oat grains

750 ml/1¼ pts/3 cups cold water
Sugar, to taste

1 Put the oats into the slow cooker and stir in the water.

2 Cover and cook on Low for 8–10 hours until the oat grains are very soft.

3 Sweeten to taste with sugar.

MAIN DISHES
WITH
VEGETABLES

It's always pleasing to know that you are getting the best of all worlds, and these recipes offer you just that. Vegetables that benefit from long, slow cooking can be left unattended to simmer until they are soft and their flavours have mingled together. Then, towards the end of cooking, or just before serving, you can quickly stir in one or two ingredients to add a touch of texture and freshness – yoghurt, cream, cheese, mustard, chopped herbs or quick-cooking vegetables such as petit pois, tomatoes or spinach. Just try these recipes and see for yourself!

Tamarind is also known as Indian date. The dark brown, slightly sticky pulp adds a sour-sweet flavour. If you like very hot spices, you could add the seeds with the chilli rings. Serve the spiced vegetables with freshly cooked rice or couscous, or popadoms and mango chutney.

spiced mixed vegetables
with tamarind and ginger

SERVES 4

15 ml/1 tbsp olive oil
5 ml/1 tsp coriander seeds
5 ml/1 tsp cumin seeds
2 garlic cloves, finely chopped
2 red chillies, sliced thinly into rings and seeded
1 small onion, thinly sliced into rings
1 large potato, cut into small dice
2 carrots, cut into small dice
450 ml/¾ pt/2 cups vegetable stock
5 ml/1 tsp ground turmeric
2.5 ml/½ tsp mixed (apple-pie) spice
2.5 ml/½ tsp ground ginger

20 ml/1½ tbsp tamarind paste or 2.5 cm/1 in square, finely chopped
425 g/15 oz/large can of chick peas (garbanzos), drained
Salt and freshly ground black pepper
1 large courgette (zucchini), cut into small dice
85 g/3 oz/¾ cup frozen petits pois
200 g/7 oz carton of plain Greek yogurt
30 ml/2 tbsp chopped fresh coriander (cilantro)

1 Preheat the slow cooker on High.

2 Heat the oil in a large pan, add the coriander and cumin seeds and cook gently, stirring, for 1 minute.

3 Add the garlic and chillies and cook gently, stirring, for 30 seconds to 1 minute.

4 Stir in the onion, potato and carrots. Increase the heat and cook for 2–3 minutes, stirring occasionally, until just beginning to brown.

5 Stir in the stock, turmeric, mixed spice, ginger and tamarind, then the chick peas and seasoning. Bring just to the boil, transfer to the slow cooker and stir gently.

6 Cover and cook on Low for 6–8 hours until everything is tender, then gently stir in the courgette, frozen petits pois and half the yogurt and cook for 30–40 minutes. All the ingredients should be very soft and tender.

7 Stir in the chopped coriander.

8 Top each serving with a swirl of the remaining yoghurt.

Harissa is an orangey-red spice mix that is used to flavour Middle Eastern dishes. It contains chillies, garlic, caraway seeds, cumin and coriander. The best way to serve these chick peas is on a bed of couscous. You could use two large cans of chick peas and omit Step 2.

tunisian-style chick peas with harissa

SERVES 4

225 g/8 oz/1⅓ cups dried chick peas (garbanzos), soaked overnight in plenty of cold water
30 ml/2 tbsp olive oil
1 onion, finely chopped
1 carrot, finely chopped
2.5 cm/1 in piece of fresh root ginger, peeled and grated
600 ml/1 pt/2½ cups vegetable stock

1 cinnamon stick
A pinch of saffron strands
30 ml/2 tbsp tomato purée (paste)
5–10 ml/1–2 tsp harissa paste
2 ripe tomatoes
Salt and freshly ground black pepper
A handful of roughly chopped fresh coriander (cilantro)

1 Preheat the slow cooker on High.

2 Drain the chick peas, put into a large pan and cover with cold water. Bring to the boil and boil gently for 10 minutes.

3 Heat the oil in a large pan, add the onion, carrot and ginger. Cook, stirring, until softened but not browned.

4 Drain the chick peas and add to the pan. Stir in the stock, cinnamon stick, saffron, tomato purée and harissa. Bring just to the boil and transfer to the slow cooker.

5 Cover and cook on Low for 8–10 hours until all the ingredients are tender.

6 Meanwhile, put the tomatoes in a bowl and cover with boiling water. Leave to stand for a minute or two before draining – the skins should then slip off easily. Discard the skins and chop the tomatoes finely. Taste and adjust the seasoning, stir in the tomatoes and coriander, then serve.

Chick peas are widely used in the cuisines of North Africa, Spain, India, the Middle East and many other countries. I just love their wonderfully rich, nutty flavour and they are delicious cooked as here in tomato sauce. Serve in bowls with basmati rice spooned on top.

spicy chick peas in tomato sauce with rosemary

SERVES 4

225 g/8 oz/1⅓ cups dried chick peas (garbanzos), soaked overnight in plenty of cold water
30 ml/2 tbsp olive oil
15 ml/1 tbsp cumin seeds
4 bay leaves
1 sprig of fresh rosemary

400 g/14 oz/large can of chopped tomatoes
2 garlic cloves, crushed
2 whole green chillies
600 ml/1 pt/2½ cups vegetable stock
30 ml/2 tbsp chopped fresh parsley or coriander (cilantro)

1 Preheat the slow cooker on High.

2 Drain the chick peas, put into a saucepan and cover with cold water. Bring to the boil and boil gently for 10 minutes.

3 Meanwhile, heat the oil in another pan, add the cumin seeds, bay leaves and rosemary and cook, stirring, for 1–2 minutes (the seeds will start to pop). Add the tomatoes, garlic, whole chillies and stock and stir.

4 Drain the chick peas and add these to the tomato mixture.

5 Bring to the boil, transfer to the slow cooker and stir gently.

6 Cover and cook on High for 8–10 hours until the chick peas are soft and tender.

7 Just before serving, stir in the parsley or coriander.

Aubergines are one of my favourite vegetables. You can find varieties with white or yellow skins, but for this recipe I would recommend using the more usual purple ones. Serve with a crisp salad and crusty bread to mop up the juices.

griddled aubergine with tomatoes and cheese

SERVES 4

400 g/14 oz/large can of tomatoes
2 garlic cloves, chopped
15 ml/1 tbsp tomato purée (paste)
15 ml/1 tbsp plain (all-purpose) flour
5 ml/1 tsp vegetable bouillon powder
5 ml/1 tsp dried oregano
50 g/2 oz Parmesan cheese, roughly chopped

3 aubergines (eggplants), about 400 g/13 oz each, thinly sliced lengthways
Olive oil, for brushing
400 g/14 oz Mozzarella cheese, thinly sliced

1 Put the all the ingredients except the aubergines, olive oil and Mozzarella into a blender or food processor, add 150 ml/¼ pt/⅔ cup of water and blend until smooth.

2 Brush the slices of aubergine lightly with olive oil. Heat a large griddle and cook the slices on both sides until softened and browned. Alternatively brown under a hot grill (broiler).

3 In the slow cooker, layer the aubergine with two-thirds of the tomato sauce and two-thirds of the slices of Mozzarella. Spread the remaining tomato sauce on top, making sure that the aubergine is covered completely

4 Cover and cook on High for 4–6 hours until the aubergine is tender.

5 Arrange the remaining Mozzarella over the top and brown lightly under the grill before serving.

This is a lovely, satisfying way to enjoy haricot beans. The black treacle gives the sauce a rich, almost smoky flavour but you could use dark muscovado sugar instead if you prefer. Serve in shallow bowls with chunks of fresh crusty bread for dipping.

spiced baked beans with treacle-tomato sauce

SERVES 4–6

225 g/8 oz/1¼ cups dried haricot (navy) beans, soaked overnight in plenty of cold water
30 ml/2 tbsp olive oil
1 onion, finely chopped
1 celery stick, finely chopped
1 large carrot, finely chopped
5 ml/1 tsp ground cumin
2 garlic cloves, finely chopped

400 g/14 oz/large can of chopped tomatoes
500 g/15 oz passata (sieved tomatoes)
45 ml/3 tbsp soy sauce
30 ml/2 tbsp black treacle (molasses)
15 ml/1 tbsp wholegrain mustard
Salt and freshly ground black pepper

1   Preheat the slow cooker on High.

2   Drain the beans, put into a pan and cover with water. Bring to the boil and boil gently for 10 minutes.

3   Meanwhile, heat the oil in a pan, add the onion, celery and carrot and cook, stirring occasionally, until softened but not browned. Add the cumin and garlic and cook, stirring, for 1–2 minutes. Add the tomatoes, passata, soy sauce, molasses and 600 ml/1 pt/2½ cups of water. Drain the beans and add them to the sauce.

4   Bring to the boil, then transfer to the slow cooker and stir gently.

5   Cover and cook on Low for 8–12 hours until the beans are very tender. Stir once or twice after the first 5 hours, if possible.

6   Stir in the mustard, add seasoning to taste, then serve.

This is an elegant vegetable dish that could be served for a special occasion. Naan bread or freshly cooked basmati rice make a perfect accompaniment to mop up the creamy aromatic sauce. Make sure you use a sweet potato with orange flesh.

aubergine, sweet potato and parsnip in coconut sauce

SERVES 4

45 ml/3 tbsp olive oil
1 large aubergine (eggplant), cut into
    dice
1 onion, chopped
15 ml/1 tbsp grated fresh root ginger
15 ml/1 tbsp garam masala
1 sweet potato, cut into dice
1 parsnip, cut into dice

425 g/15 oz/large can of chick peas
    (garbanzos), drained
400 g/14 oz/large can of chopped
    tomatoes
350 ml/12 fl oz/1½ cups coconut milk
Salt and freshly ground black pepper

1 Preheat the slow cooker on High.

2 Heat the oil in a large pan, add the aubergine and onion and cook, stirring occasionally, until soft and golden brown.

3 Stir in the root ginger and garam masala.

4 Add the remaining ingredients and bring to the boil. Transfer to the slow cooker and stir gently.

5 Cover and cook on Low for 7–9 hours until everything is tender.

6 Stir well before serving.

This curry is just bursting with flavours and the combination of spinach and nuts brings an interesting texture. You could use more chillies if you like a fiery dish. Basmati rice and mango chutney are all that are required to make a simple but satisfying meal.

red bean, cashew and spinach curry

SERVES 4

15 ml/1 tbsp olive oil
1 large onion, finely chopped
1 large carrot, finely chopped
5 ml/1 tsp ground cumin
5 ml/1 tsp ground coriander
2.5 ml/½ tsp ground turmeric
15 ml/1 tbsp grated fresh root ginger
2 green chillies, finely chopped

2 garlic cloves, finely chopped
425 g/15 oz/large can of red kidney
    beans, drained
50 g/2 oz/½ cup ground almonds
75 g/3 oz/¾ cup unsalted cashew
    nuts
2 large handfuls of baby spinach
    leaves

1 Preheat the slow cooker on High.

2 Heat the oil in a pan, add the onion and carrot and cook, stirring occasionally, until slightly softened but not browned.

3 Add the spices, root ginger, chillies and garlic and cook, stirring, for 1–2 minutes.

4 Stir in the beans, almonds, cashew nuts and 300 ml/½ pt/1¼ cups of water and bring just to the boil. Transfer to the slow cooker and stir gently.

5 Cover and cook on Low for 6–8 hours until the ingredients are tender.

6 When you are ready to serve, add the spinach and stir until just wilted, then serve immediately.

Serve this on a bed of hot rice – basmati if you have it. If you prefer the chestnuts to retain some 'bite', don't add them at the start but stir them into the sauce 30–40 minutes before serving. Remember that heat is lost when you open the slow cooker, so make sure you do this quickly.

mushroom, chestnut and onion stroganoff

SERVES 4

15 ml/1 tbsp olive oil
25 g/1 oz/2 tbsp butter or margarine
1 large onion, thinly sliced
1 large garlic clove, finely chopped
350 g/12 oz chestnut mushrooms, halved or quartered
240 g/9 oz/small can of peeled chestnuts

300 ml/½ pt/1¼ cups vegetable stock
15 ml/1 tbsp mushroom ketchup (catsup)
15 ml/1 tbsp Dijon mustard
30 ml/2 tbsp crème fraîche

1 Preheat the slow cooker on High.

2 Heat the oil and butter or margarine in a pan, add the onion and garlic and cook, stirring occasionally, until slightly softened but not browned.

3 Put the mushrooms and chestnuts into the slow cooker.

4 Add the stock and mushroom ketchup to the pan of onions.

5 Bring just to the boil and pour over the mushrooms in the slow cooker. Stir gently and level the surface.

6 Cover and cook on Low for 6–8 hours until very tender, then stir in the mustard and crème fraîche and cook for a further 30 minutes, then serve.

Acorn squash would work just as successfully in this dish, but you could use mixed root vegetables such as carrots, swedes and parsnips. These are all winter vegetables, so this is an ideal dish for those long, cold evenings when you really crave some comfort food!

gingered butternut squash with cheese toasts

SERVES 4

1 butternut squash (about 900 g/
   2 lb), peeled, seeded and cut into
   cubes
15 ml/1 tbsp olive oil
1 onion, finely chopped
1 garlic clove, finely chopped
2.5 cm/1 in piece of fresh root ginger,
   peeled and finely grated

450 ml/¾ pt/2 cups vegetable stock
Salt and freshly ground black pepper
8 small thick slices of rustic bread,
   such as ciabatta
50 ml/2 oz/½ cup grated Cheddar or
   Gruyère (Swiss) cheese

1 Put the squash into the slow cooker.

2 Heat the oil in a pan, add the onion, garlic and ginger and cook, stirring occasionally, until slightly softened but not browned.

3 Add the stock and seasoning to the pan.

4 Bring just to the boil and pour over the squash in the slow cooker. Stir gently and level the surface. If necessary, add a little more stock so that the squash is just covered.

5 Cover and cook on Low for 6–10 hours until the squash is very tender.

6 When ready to serve, toast the bread slices, top with cheese and grill (broil) until bubbling and golden.

7 Serve the squash with the cheese toasts.

Depending on the season and availability of ingredients, I might replace the aubergine and pepper with winter vegetables such as swede, parsnip and celeriac. The dumplings make this a hearty and satisfying dish that is a particular favourite with my family.

vegetable casserole with thyme and cheese dumplings

SERVES 4

15 ml/1 tbsp olive oil
1 large onion, thinly sliced
1 large leek, thinly sliced
225 g/8 oz baby carrots, halved
    lengthways
225 g/8 oz baby new potatoes, thickly
    sliced
1 small aubergine (eggplant), cut into
    cubes
1 red (bell) pepper, thinly sliced
750 ml/1¼ pts/3 cups vegetable stock
Finely grated zest and juice of 1 small
    orange

15 ml/1 tbsp clear honey
5 ml/1 tsp ground cinnamon
Salt and freshly ground pepper

FOR THE DUMPLINGS
100 g/4 oz/1 cup self-raising (self-
    rising) flour
5 ml/1 tsp baking powder
5 ml/1 tsp dried thyme
50 g/2 oz/½ cup chopped (shredded)
    vegetable suet
Salt and freshly ground black pepper
50 g/2 oz mature Cheddar cheese,
    cut into 8 small cubes

1 Preheat the slow cooker on High.

2 Heat the oil in a large pan, add the vegetables and cook, stirring occasionally, until slightly softened and just beginning to brown.

3 Add the stock, orange zest and juice, honey, cinnamon and seasoning.

4 Bring to the boil, transfer to the slow cooker and stir gently, pushing the vegetables into the liquid.

5 Cover and cook on Low for 6–9 hours or until the vegetables are tender.

6 Meanwhile, make the dumplings. Sift the flour with the baking powder and stir in the thyme, suet and seasoning. Stir in sufficient cold water to make a firm dough. Divide the mixture into eight balls. Press a cube of cheese into the centre of each ball, gathering the dough around it and pinching the edges together to seal it.

7 Switch the slow cooker to High. Stir the casserole gently. Arrange the dumplings on top of the vegetables. Cover and cook for 30–40 minutes until the dumplings are puffed up.

8 Serve immediately.

Don't worry about the number of ingredients – this curry couldn't be simpler to make! I often use thinly sliced carrots and fennel, small cauliflower florets and small cubes of sweet potato and parsnip but you can use whatever vegetables you like. Serve with basmati rice or naan bread.

creamy-sweet vegetable tikka masala

SERVES 4–6

25 g/1 oz/2 tbsp ghee, butter or margarine
1 onion, thinly sliced
15 ml/1 tbsp tikka blend curry powder
10 ml/2 tsp ground coriander
2.5 ml/½ tsp ground paprika
2.5 ml/½ tsp ground turmeric
1.5 ml/¼ tsp chilli powder
5 ml/1 tsp salt
1 small red (bell) pepper, sliced
750 g/1¾ lb mixed vegetables
2 large garlic cloves, finely chopped

1 green chilli, seeded and finely chopped
15 ml/1 tbsp grated fresh root ginger
30 ml/2 tbsp plain yoghurt
15 ml/1 tbsp lemon juice
300 ml/½ pt/1¼ cups vegetable stock
250 ml/9 fl oz/1 cup passata (sieved tomatoes)
50 g/2 oz/½ cup ground almonds
30–45 ml/2–3 tbsp double (heavy) cream
60 ml/4 tbsp chopped fresh coriander (cilantro)

1 Preheat the slow cooker on High.

2 Melt the ghee, butter or margarine in a large pan, add the onion and cook, stirring occasionally, until slightly softened but not browned.

3 Stir in the spices and salt and cook, stirring, for 1 minute.

4 Add all the remaining ingredients except the almonds, cream and fresh coriander. Bring to the boil.

5 Stir in the almonds and transfer to the slow cooker.

6 Stir gently, cover and cook on Low for 7–10 hours, stirring gently once or twice after the first 4 hours if possible. All the ingredients should be very tender.

7 When ready to serve, stir in the cream and fresh coriander.

MAIN DISHES WITH PASTA AND GRAINS

This section contains some of my favourite recipes. Those familiar staples, rice and pasta, are here of course – they are always very popular and seem to go down particularly well with children. But I have also included some less well–known grains, such as couscous, whole wheat and quinoa, which I am sure you will enjoy just as much.

In addition, you will find dishes using barley, buckwheat and bulghar (cracked wheat) in the chapters on Soups (see page 29) and Starters, Side Dishes and Light Meals (see page 42).

The brown rice and kidney beans in this recipe make this an extremely healthy and nutritious meal. It is good served with just a crisp green salad and it also makes a great accompaniment to vegetable kebabs or just about anything prepared on the barbecue.

brown rice with tomato and red kidney beans

SERVES 4

15 ml/1 tbsp olive oil
1 onion, finely chopped
225 g/8 oz/1 cup easy-cook brown
   rice
750 ml/1¼ pts/3 cups vegetable stock
425 g/15 oz/large can of red kidney
   beans, drained

30 ml/2 tbsp tomato purée (paste)
5 ml/1 tsp harissa paste or chilli
   sauce
1 red (bell) pepper, cut into small dice
A small handful of toasted flaked
   (slivered) almonds

1 Preheat the slow cooker on High.

2 Heat the oil in a pan, add the onion and cook, stirring occasionally, until softened and golden brown.

3 Stir in the rice, stock, beans, tomato purée and harissa paste or chilli sauce. Bring just to the boil, transfer to the slow cooker and stir gently.

4 Cover and cook on High for 1 hour, then gently stir in the red pepper. Cook for a further 20–30 minutes or until the rice is tender.

5 Serve sprinkled with toasted flaked almonds.

This is a deliciously refreshing and fruity rice dish. It is very good when served with roasted vegetables or crisply fried onions and some black olives. Alternatively, it goes well with many of the spicy recipes in this book, particularly those that use quorn.

brown rice with fennel, orange and raisins

SERVES 4

225 g/8 oz/1 cup easy-cook brown rice
1 small fennel bulb, trimmed and thinly sliced
50 g/2 oz/⅓ cup raisins
10 ml/2 tsp ground coriander
300 ml/½ pt/1¼ cups orange juice
Salt and freshly ground black pepper
30 ml/2 tbsp olive oil
15 ml/1 tbsp snipped fresh chives
1 orange, peeled and cut into segments

1 Preheat the slow cooker on High.

2 Put the rice into a pan and add the fennel, raisins, coriander, orange juice and seasoning. Stir in 450 ml/¾ pt/2 cups of water. Bring just to the boil, transfer to the slow cooker and stir gently.

3 Cover and cook on High for 1–1½ hours, stirring gently after 1 hour, until the rice is tender.

4 Just before serving, gently stir in the olive oil, chives and orange segments.

Sugar snap peas and asparagus feature in this recipe but other vegetables in season, such as courgettes, beans or carrots, would be just as nice. Whatever you choose, slice or cut them into small pieces so that they can be quickly stir-fried or steamed just before serving.

rice with chick peas and spring vegetables

SERVES 4

15 ml/1 tbsp olive oil, plus extra for
   drizzling
1 small onion, thinly sliced
1 garlic clove, finely chopped
225 g/8 oz/1 cup easy-cook long-
   grain rice and wild rice mix
750 ml/1¼ pts/3 cups vegetable stock
150 ml/¼ pt/⅔ cup apple juice
5 ml/1 tsp sweet chilli sauce

1 red or orange (bell) pepper,
   chopped
425 g/15 oz/large can of chick peas
   (garbanzos), drained
Salt and freshly ground black pepper
100 g/4 oz sugar snap peas
100 g/4 oz asparagus tips
15 ml/1 tbsp chopped fresh parsley

1 Preheat the slow cooker on High.

2 Heat the oil in a pan, add the onion and garlic and cook gently, stirring occasionally, until softened but not browned.

3 Stir in the rice and cook for 1 minute.

4 Add the stock, apple juice, chilli sauce, pepper, chick peas and a little seasoning. Bring just to the boil and transfer to the slow cooker.

5 Cover and cook on High for 1½–2 hours, stirring gently after 1 hour, until all the liquid has been absorbed and the rice is tender.

6 Either stir-fry the vegetables in a little oil or steam them lightly – they should still have some 'bite'.

7 Sprinkle the rice with the parsley, top with the vegetables and drizzle with some extra olive oil, then serve.

Couscous is a wonderfully useful storecupboard stand-by. It is quick to cook and needs to be added to the crock pot for only the last 5–10 minutes to fluff up. It's best to use ordinary dried apricots, not the ready-to-eat variety. The pine nuts add a lovely texture to the dish.

spiced couscous with apricots, feta and pine nuts

SERVES 4

30 ml/2 tbsp olive oil, plus extra for drizzling
2 onions, thinly sliced
1 garlic clove, finely chopped
600 ml/1 pt/2½ cups vegetable stock
5 ml/1 tsp ground mixed (apple-pie) spice
Freshly ground black pepper

100 g/4 oz/⅔ cup dried apricots, quartered
225 g/8 oz/2 cups couscous
225 g/8 oz feta cheese, cubed
30 ml/2 tbsp chopped fresh parsley
25 g/1 oz/¼ cup pine nuts

1 Preheat the slow cooker on High.

2 Heat the oil in a pan, add the onions and garlic and cook, stirring frequently, until softened and golden brown.

3 Stir in the stock, spice, seasoning and apricots. Bring just to the boil and transfer to the slow cooker.

4 Cover and cook on Low for 4–6 hours until all the ingredients are tender.

5 Stir in the couscous, cover and cook for a further 5–10 minutes until all the liquid has been absorbed and the couscous is tender.

6 Gently stir in the feta cheese and parsley, cover and leave to stand for about 5 minutes.

7 Serve immediately, topped with pine nuts and drizzled with a little extra olive oil.

This recipe is full of all those ingredients that are associated with the flavour of the Orient. Ready-cooked 'stir-in' noodles are ideal for this dish, or you could cook some of your favourite kind and drain them before adding to the crock pot for the final 30 minutes.

oriental noodles with spring onions and bamboo shoots

SERVES 4

4 large spring onions (scallions)
15 g/½ oz dried oyster mushrooms
4 cm/1½ in piece of fresh root ginger
1 small red (bell) pepper, thinly sliced
250 g/9 oz/small can of sliced bamboo shoots and water chestnuts, drained

1 litre/1¾ pts/4¼ cups vegetable stock
60 ml/4 tbsp soy sauce
2.5 ml/½ tsp sweet chilli sauce
5 ml/1 tsp sugar
300 g/11 oz packet of cooked 'stir-in' noodles
A handful of fresh beansprouts

1   Thinly slice the white parts of the spring onions, reserving the green parts, and put into the slow cooker.

2   Wash, drain and chop the mushrooms and add to the slow cooker.

3   Roughly grate the ginger, skin and all. Gather the gratings in one hand and, holding them over the slow cooker, squeeze tightly so that the juice runs out through your fingers into the mixture. Once every last drop has been squeezed out, discard the gratings.

4   Add the pepper, bamboo shoots and water chestnuts, stock, soy sauce, chilli sauce and sugar.

5   Cover and cook on Low for 6–8 hours until the vegetables are tender. Add the noodles, beansprouts and reserved green onion and cook for a further 30–40 minutes until the noodles are hot.

6   Serve immediately in shallow bowls.

This lovely nutty flavoured dish is best when the grains are just cooked and there is still some soup-like liquid. Risottos can be time-consuming when cooked the conventional way, but in the slow cooker they can be left to cook to perfection on their own!

brown rice risotto with leek, mushrooms and parmesan

SERVES 4

15 ml/1 tbsp olive oil
25 g/1 oz/2 tbsp butter or margarine
1 leek, thinly sliced
1 garlic clove, finely chopped
225 g/8 oz/1 cup easy-cook brown
   rice

750 ml/1¼ pts/3 cups vegetable stock
225 g/8 oz chestnut mushrooms,
   thickly sliced or quartered
Shavings of Parmesan cheese, to
   garnish

1 Preheat the slow cooker on High.

2 Heat the oil and butter or margarine in a pan, add the leek and garlic and cook, stirring occasionally, until softened but not browned.

3 Stir in the rice, then add the stock and mushrooms and bring just to the boil. Transfer to the slow cooker and stir gently.

4 Cover and cook on High for 1–1½ hours, stirring gently after 1 hour, until the vegetables are tender and the rice is just soft.

5 Serve topped with shavings of Parmesan cheese.

This is a versatile salad because you can adjust which herbs you add to suit the rest of the meal. It is also good served cold – stir the dressing and herbs into the hot wheat, then leave to cool before tossing in the cheese cubes and topping with Parmesan shavings.

hot wheat salad with fresh herbs and cheese

SERVES 4

225 g/8 oz/2 cups whole precooked durum wheat grains
750 ml/1¼ pts/3 cups hot vegetable stock
45 ml/3 tbsp olive oil
15 ml/1 tbsp white wine vinegar or lemon juice
7.5 ml/1½ tsp wholegrain mustard
5 ml/1 tsp sugar

A handful of chopped mixed fresh herbs, such as basil, parsley and coriander (cilantro)
225 g/8 oz cheese, such as feta or Cheddar, cut into cubes
Shavings of Parmesan cheese, to garnish

1 Put the wheat into the slow cooker and add the hot vegetable stock, stirring.

2 Cover and cook on High for 1¼–2 hours or until the wheat is tender.

3 Meanwhile, whisk together the oil, vinegar or lemon juice, mustard and sugar to make the dressing.

4 Drain the wheat and toss with the dressing, herbs and cheese cubes.

5 Serve topped with shavings of Parmesan cheese.

*Gremolata is a delicious, fresh-tasting garnish made with finely
grated lemon zest, crushed garlic and finely chopped fresh parsley.
Chunks of fresh, crusty bread – preferably a rustic kind – are the
only accompaniments needed to make this a substantial dinner dish.*

butter bean and pasta casserole with gremolata

SERVES 6

15 g/½ oz dried mushrooms, such as
   oyster or porcini
225 g/8 oz/1¼ cups dried butter
   (lima) beans, soaked overnight in
   cold water
15 ml/1 tbsp olive oil
1 onion, finely chopped
1 garlic clove, finely chopped
1 large leek, sliced
400 g/14 oz/large can of chopped
   tomatoes

5 ml/1 tsp dried oregano
750 ml/1¼ pts/3 cups vegetable stock
Salt and freshly ground black pepper
A small handful of dried pasta shapes

FOR THE GREMOLATA
Finely grated zest of 1 lemon
60 ml/4 tbsp finely chopped fresh
   parsley
2 garlic cloves, crushed

1   Pour 300 ml/½ pt/1¼ cups of boiling water over the mushrooms and
    leave to stand for 20–30 minutes. Strain, reserving the liquid, and
    chop the mushrooms.

2   Drain the soaked beans, put into a large pan and cover with cold
    water. Bring to the boil and boil gently for 10 minutes.

3   Meanwhile, heat the oil in a large pan, then add the onion, garlic
    and leek. Cook, stirring occasionally, until softened but not
    browned. Stir in the tomatoes, oregano, mushrooms, stock and the
    reserved mushroom liquid. Season lightly with salt and pepper.

4   Bring just to the boil and transfer to the slow cooker.

5   Cover and cook on Low for 6–8 hours until all the vegetables are
    tender, then stir in the pasta and cook for a further 30 minutes or
    until soft.

6   Meanwhile, mix together the gremolata ingredients.

7   Check the casserole and adjust the seasoning to taste. Ladle the
    mixture into shallow bowls and sprinkle the gremolata on top.

This might not seem a big enough quantity of quinoa to serve four, but remember that it expands a great deal during cooking. Take care not to overcook it – you don't want to end up with a paste. The eggs are wrapped in foil and cooked in the slow cooker with the other ingredients.

hot quinoa, tomato and egg salad

SERVES 4

4 eggs
200 g/7 oz/scant 1 cup quinoa
50 g/2 oz/½ cup semi-dried tomatoes, chopped
650 ml/22 fl oz/2¾ cups vegetable stock

Freshly ground black pepper
45 ml/3 tbsp olive oil
15 ml/1 tbsp lemon juice
A small handful of fresh basil leaves

1 Wrap each egg tightly in foil.

2 Put the quinoa and tomatoes into the slow cooker and stir in the stock. Season with pepper and add the eggs in their foil.

3 Cover and cook on High for 1–1½ hours or until the quinoa has just absorbed all the liquid.

4 Lift the eggs out and remove the foil. Shell the eggs under cold, running water and cut into halves or quarters.

5 Gently stir the oil, lemon juice and basil leaves into the hot mixture.

6 Pile on warm plates and serve topped with the eggs.

This dish works best in a slow cooker with a wide top, such as an oval. It cooks perfectly in this way and just needs browning under a hot grill to finish it. I like to have plenty of cheese sauce on the top but you could use less if you prefer. Serve with a crisp salad.

courgette and roasted pepper lasagne

SERVES 4–6

30 ml/2 tbsp olive oil, plus extra for greasing
1 large onion, finely chopped
2 garlic cloves, finely chopped
400 g/14 oz/large can of chopped tomatoes
200 ml/7 fl oz/¾ cup vegetable stock
10 ml/2 tsp dried mixed herbs
Salt and freshly ground black pepper
4 courgettes (zucchini), coarsely grated
290 g/10½ oz jar of roasted peppers in brine, drained and thinly sliced

60 ml/4 tbsp freshly grated Parmesan cheese, plus extra for topping
12 sheets of fresh lasagne

FOR THE CHEESE SAUCE
450 ml/¾ pt/2 cups milk
25 g/1 oz/2 tbsp butter or margarine
25 g/1 oz/¼ cup plain (all-purpose) flour
75 g/3 oz/¾ cup grated mature cheese, such as Cheddar

1   Heat the oil in a pan, add the onion and garlic and cook, stirring gently, until softened but not browned.

2   Add the tomatoes, stock, herbs and seasoning. Bring to the boil and bubble gently for 2–3 minutes. Stir in the courgettes and peppers and remove from the heat.

3   Oil the inside of the slow cooker.

4   Layer the sheets of lasagne and the vegetable sauce in the slow cooker, scattering the Parmesan in between and finishing with a layer of sauce. Make sure the sauce coats the pasta completely.

5   Cover and cook on High for 2–4 hours until soft throughout.

6 Make the cheese sauce. Put the milk into a saucepan with the butter and flour. Stirring with a whisk, bring the mixture to the boil, until thickened and smooth, then bubble gently for 1–2 minutes. Season to taste with salt and pepper and stir in the grated cheese.

7 Lift the slow cooker pot out of its casing and pour the sauce over the lasagne, spreading it to the edges.

8 Sprinkle with a little extra Parmesan cheese and put under a hot grill (broiler) or in a hot oven until the top is bubbling and golden brown.

9 Leave to stand for 10 minutes before serving.

Risottos made in the slow cooker are so easy because you don't have to stand over a pan, stirring. Even such a small weight of dried porcini mushrooms gives an intense flavour to this risotto. For an extra-special touch, try replacing 60 ml/4 tbsp of the stock with white wine.

easy-cook mushroom and cheese risotto

SERVES 4

20 g/¾ oz dried porcini mushrooms
15 ml/1 tbsp olive oil
25 g/1 oz/2 tbsp butter or margarine
1 onion, finely chopped
1 garlic clove, finely chopped
225 g/8 oz/1 cup easy-cook long-grain rice

225 g/8 oz chestnut mushrooms, thinly sliced
450 ml/¾ pt/2 cups vegetable stock
Salt and freshly ground black pepper
45 ml/3 tbsp freshly grated Parmesan cheese, plus extra for topping
45 ml/3 tbsp chopped fresh herbs, such as chives or parsley

1   Put the dried mushrooms in a bowl, pour over 150 ml/¼ pt/⅔ cup of boiling water and leave to stand for 15 minutes. Drain, reserving the liquid, and finely chop the mushrooms.

2   Preheat the slow cooker on High.

3   Heat the oil and butter in a large pan, add the onion and garlic and cook, stirring occasionally, until softened but not browned.

4   Stir in the rice, then the fresh and soaked mushrooms.

5   Add the stock and seasoning and bring just to the boil. Transfer to the slow cooker and stir gently.

6   Cover and cook on High for 1 hour, stir gently, then cook for a further 30 minutes until the rice is cooked through and the risotto is creamy.

7   Just before serving, stir in the Parmesan cheese and herbs.

8   Serve sprinkled with extra Parmesan cheese.

MAIN DISHES WITH TOFU AND QUORN

I have compiled this section in response to readers who have written to ask if they can use tofu and Quorn in their slow cooker. The simple answer is a resounding 'Yes', as these recipes show. Both tofu and Quorn stay beautifully firm and retain their unique texture while absorbing flavours from all the other ingredients in the pot. I hope these dishes will inspire you to make more use of both of them.

The sweetness of the cooked root vegetables is complemented perfectly by the delicate fragrance of coconut. You could be creative and vary the vegetables. I like to serve this with plain boiled rice sprinkled with chopped fresh coriander.

root vegetables and tofu in spiced coconut sauce

SERVES 4

15 ml/1 tbsp olive oil, plus extra for cooking
1 large onion, thinly sliced
2 garlic cloves, finely chopped
30 ml/2 tbsp finely chopped fresh root ginger
15 ml/1 tbsp curry paste
5 ml/1 tsp ground turmeric
1.5 ml/¼ tsp chilli powder
300 ml/½ pt/1¼ cups vegetable stock

450 g/1 lb swede (rutabaga), peeled and cut into cubes
1 large carrot, thinly sliced
1 parsnip, thinly sliced
Salt and freshly ground black pepper
200 ml/7 fl oz/small carton of coconut cream
About 225 g/8 oz firm tofu, dried and sliced
30 ml/2 tbsp soy sauce

1 Preheat the slow cooker on High.

2 Heat the oil in a large pan, add the onion, garlic and ginger and cook, stirring occasionally, until softened but not browned.

3 Stir in the curry paste, turmeric and chilli.

4 Add the stock, swede, carrot, parsnip and seasoning.

5 Bring just to the boil, transfer to the slow cooker and stir gently, pushing the vegetables into the sauce.

6 Cover and cook on Low for 6–8 hours until tender, then add the coconut cream and cook for a further 30 minutes.

7 Meanwhile, stir the tofu slices into the soy sauce and leave to stand for 30 minutes.

8 When ready to serve, heat a little oil in a frying pan (skillet), add the tofu, a few pieces at a time, and cook quickly until browned and crisp on both sides.

9 Serve the vegetables and sauce topped with the crispy tofu.

You can leave the tofu plain, in which case omit Step 3, but I like to brown it first – preferably on a griddle pan because the stripes it makes are so attractive. The peppercorns could be replaced with capers, which would impart an equally pungent flavour.

tofu on beans and tomatoes with peppercorns

SERVES 2

425 g/15 oz/large can of flageolet beans, drained
200 g/7 oz/small can of sweetcorn (corn), drained
4 large spring onions (scallions), thinly sliced
2 large ripe tomatoes, thinly sliced
5 ml/1 tsp green peppercorns
30 ml/2 tbsp white wine
15 ml/1 tbsp extra virgin olive oil
250 g/9 oz packet of marinated or smoked firm tofu, drained, dried and cut into long strips
30 ml/2 tbsp chopped fresh herbs, such as mint or parsley

1   Arrange the beans, sweetcorn and onion in the bottom of the slow cooker. Lay the tomatoes on top and scatter the peppercorns over. Add the wine.

2   Preheat the slow cooker on High.

3   Meanwhile, heat the oil in a frying pan (skillet), add the tofu and brown quickly on both sides.

4   Transfer the browned tofu to the slow cooker.

5   Cover and cook on High for 2–2½ hours or until all the ingredients are piping hot.

6   Just before serving, scatter the herbs over the top.

Ordinary tomatoes are fine for this recipe but good cherry tomatoes would give even more flavour. Or, if you need to cut a couple of corners, using a 400 g/14 oz/large can of chopped tomatoes would also be perfectly acceptable and you can omit Step 2.

smoked tofu
in fresh tomato sauce

SERVES 4

225 g/8 oz ripe tomatoes
15 ml/1 tbsp olive oil
1 small onion, finely chopped
1 garlic clove, finely chopped
1 small carrot, finely chopped
1 small celery stick, finely chopped
15 ml/1 tbsp plain (all-purpose) flour

300 ml/½ pt/1¼ cups vegetable stock
5 ml/1 tsp sugar
5 ml/1 tsp dried oregano
Salt and freshly ground black pepper
250 g/9 oz packet of smoked firm
   tofu, drained, dried and cut into
   cubes

1 Preheat the slow cooker on High.

2 Put the tomatoes in a bowl and pour over sufficient boiling water to cover them completely. Leave to stand for 5 minutes, after which the skins should slip off easily. Finely chop the tomatoes.

3 Heat the oil in a pan, add the onion, garlic, carrot and celery and cook, stirring occasionally, until softened and just beginning to brown.

4 Stir in the flour, then gradually stir in the stock. Add the tomatoes, sugar, oregano and seasoning.

5 Bring just to the boil, transfer to the slow cooker and stir gently.

6 Cover and cook on Low for 4–6 hours until the vegetables are tender, then stir in the tofu and cook for a further 30 minutes.

7 Check and adjust the seasoning to taste before serving.

This is a light, Mediterranean-style dish that only needs to be served with crusty bread to mop up the juices to make a satisfying main meal. It can also be served as a starter, in which case the quantity here would be enough for four people. Use marinated, smoked or plain tofu.

tofu and vegetables in a white wine sauce

SERVES 2

1 red onion, thinly sliced
1 yellow (bell) pepper, thinly sliced
1 bunch of asparagus, tough stalks
   removed, cut into 4 cm/1½ in
   lengths
8 cherry tomatoes, halved
Salt and freshly ground black pepper

5 ml/1 tsp dried oregano
About 16 black olives
120 ml/4 fl oz/½ cup white wine
250 g/9 oz packet of firm tofu,
   drained, dried and cut into cubes
30 ml/2 tbsp extra-virgin olive oil

1 Preheat the slow cooker on High while you prepare the ingredients.

2 Scatter the onion in the bottom of the slow cooker, followed by the pepper, asparagus and tomatoes.

3 Season with salt and pepper and sprinkle the oregano over. Add the olives.

4 Heat the wine in a small pan until it just comes to the boil, then pour over the vegetables.

5 Cover and cook on High for 2–2½ hours, stirring in the tofu after 1 hour, until all the ingredients are soft.

6 Just before serving, adjust the seasoning to taste and drizzle the olive oil over.

I devised this recipe in response to a friend's request for a vegetarian cassoulet. It is a nutritious and hearty dish that I feel has all the texture and flavour you would expect from a more traditional cassoulet containing meat. Serve with a crisp green salad.

vegetarian cassoulet
with tofu and haricot beans

SERVES 4

15 ml/1 tbsp olive oil
1 large onion, thinly sliced
2 large celery sticks, thinly sliced
2 garlic cloves, finely chopped
300 ml/½ pt/1¼ cups vegetable stock
20 ml/generous 1 tbsp black treacle (molasses)
15 ml/1 tbsp wholegrain mustard
Salt and freshly ground black pepper

2 x 425 g/15 oz/large cans of haricot (navy) beans, drained
250 g/9 oz packet of marinated tofu, cut into cubes
4 vegetarian sausages made with tofu, thickly sliced
25 g/1 oz/2 tbsp butter or margarine
90 ml/6 tbsp fresh breadcrumbs

1 Preheat the slow cooker on High.

2 Heat the oil in a large pan and add the onion, celery and garlic. Cook, stirring occasionally, until softened and beginning to brown.

3 Stir in the stock, treacle, mustard, seasoning and beans and bring just to the boil. Put the tofu and sausage slices into the slow cooker and pour the bean mixture over. Stir gently, making sure that the liquid covers the ingredients.

4 Cover and cook on Low for 4–6 hours until everything is tender. Stir once or twice during the final 1–1½ hours.

5 Meanwhile, melt the butter or margarine in a frying pan (skillet), add the breadcrumbs and cook, stirring occasionally, until crisp and golden brown. Set aside.

6 Serve the cassoulet on warm plates, topped with some crisp breadcrumbs.

Quorn itself has a bland flavour, but here it takes on the flavour of all the other ingredients to make a delicious Bolognese-style dish. Serve it on a bed of freshly cooked spaghetti, topped with flakes of full-flavoured hard cheese such as Parmesan.

quorn and fresh vegetable bolognese

SERVES 4

15 ml/1 tbsp olive oil
1 onion, finely chopped
1 large carrot, finely chopped
1 leek, thinly sliced
1 garlic clove, finely chopped
1 red (bell) pepper, cut into dice
1 yellow pepper, cut into dice
400 g/14 oz/large can of chopped
   tomatoes

300 ml/½ pt/1¼ cups vegetable stock
30 ml/2 tbsp tomato purée (paste)
15 ml/1 tbsp mushroom ketchup
   (catsup)
15 ml/1 tbsp soy sauce
5 ml/1 tsp dried oregano or thyme
300 g/11 oz packet of minced
   (ground) Quorn, thawed if
   frozen

1   Preheat the slow cooker on High.

2   Heat the oil in a large pan and add the onion, carrot and leek. Cook, stirring occasionally, until softened and just beginning to brown.

3   Stir in the garlic and peppers.

4   Add the tomatoes, stock, tomato purée, mushroom ketchup, soy sauce and herbs.

5   Bring just to the boil, transfer to the slow cooker and stir gently.

6   Cover and cook on Low for 6–7 hours or until all of the ingredients are tender. Stir in the Quorn and cook for a further 1 hour, then serve.

Thai green curry has become so popular in recent years, and this recipe proves that a vegetarian version can have all the flavour you would expect. Serve this in bowls with freshly cooked Thai fragrant rice and a generous garnishing of chopped coriander.

thai green curry
with quorn

SERVES 4

15 ml/1 tbsp olive oil
1 large onion, thinly sliced
1 carrot, thinly sliced
2 celery sticks, sliced
1 red (bell) pepper, sliced
15 ml/1 tbsp Thai green curry paste
1 garlic clove, finely chopped
2.5 cm/1 in piece of fresh root ginger, peeled and finely chopped
300 ml/½ pt/1¼ cups vegetable stock
100 g/4 oz green beans, halved crossways

30 ml/2 tbsp soy sauce
Finely grated zest and juice of 1 lime
400 g/14 oz/large can of coconut milk
2 x 300 g/11 oz packets of Quorn pieces, thawed if frozen
100 g/4 oz courgettes (zucchini), sliced
100 g/4 oz mangetout (snow peas)
A handful of roughly chopped fresh coriander (cilantro)

1 Preheat the slow cooker on High.

2 Heat the oil in a large pan and add the onion, carrot, celery and pepper. Cook, stirring occasionally, until slightly softened but not browned.

3 Stir in the curry paste, garlic and ginger and cook, stirring, for 1–2 minutes.

4 Add the stock, beans, soy sauce and lime zest and juice. Bring just to the boil, transfer to the slow cooker and stir.

5 Cover and cook on Low for 4–6 hours or until all the vegetables are tender. Stir in the coconut milk, Quorn, courgettes and mangetout and cook for a further 1 hour.

6 Serve hot, garnished with chopped coriander.

Serve this in a bowl with garlic bread on the side, on a bed of plain boiled long-grain rice, or as a filling for jacket potatoes. The amount of chilli I give here will certainly provide a noticeable spicy heat, but you can add less – or more! – to suit your own taste.

vegetable chilli
with quorn

SERVES 4

15 ml/1 tbsp olive oil
1 onion, finely chopped
1 small carrot, finely chopped
1 celery stick, finely chopped
1 garlic clove, finely chopped
400 g/14 oz/large can of chopped
   tomatoes
300 ml/½ pt/1¼ cups vegetable stock

15 ml/1 tbsp tomato purée (paste)
1 red (bell) pepper, thinly sliced
2.5 ml/½ tsp crushed dried chillies
225 g/8 oz/small can of red kidney
   beans, drained
300 g/11 oz packet of minced
   (ground) Quorn, thawed if frozen

1 Preheat the slow cooker on High.

2 Heat the oil in a pan and add the onion, carrot, celery and garlic. Cook, stirring occasionally, until softened but not browned.

3 Stir in the remaining ingredients.

4 Bring just to the boil, transfer to the slow cooker and stir gently.

5 Cover and cook on Low for 5–7 hours until all the ingredients are tender.

6 Stir well before serving.

This recipe works equally well using cubes of firm tofu, especially the marinated variety. Serve it on a bed of freshly cooked rice. If you do a lot of Chinese-style cookery, you may have a bottle of hoisin sauce in your storecupboard, in which case use it instead of the sherry.

quorn in sweet and sour sauce

SERVES 4

15 ml/1 tbsp olive oil
1 onion, thinly sliced
1 garlic clove, finely chopped
1 carrot, thinly sliced
30 ml/2 tbsp cornflour (cornstarch)
60 ml/4 tbsp soy sauce
30 ml/2 tbsp dry sherry
30 ml/2 tbsp white wine vinegar
300 ml/½ pt/1¼ cups vegetable stock

225 g/8 oz/small can of pineapple
   pieces in natural juice
1 small yellow (bell) pepper, thinly
   sliced
1 small green pepper, thinly sliced
300 g/11 oz/packet of Quorn pieces,
   thawed if frozen
Freshly ground black pepper

1 Preheat the slow cooker on High.

2 Heat the oil in a pan and add the onion, garlic and carrot. Cook, stirring occasionally, until softened but not browned.

3 Stir in the cornflour, then gradually stir in the soy sauce, sherry, wine vinegar and stock. Add the pineapple and its juice.

4 Bring just to the boil, transfer to the slow cooker and stir gently.

5 Cover and cook on Low for 3½–5 hours or until tender. Stir in the remaining ingredients and cook for a further 1 hour until the pepper is soft, then serve.

The sweet potatoes, chick peas and quorn in this recipe are beautifully flavoured by the ginger, dried spices and lemon to produce a satisfying dish with a hint of the Middle East. It is simplicity itself to prepare, and just needs the accompaniment of freshly cooked couscous.

moroccan-style quorn with sweet potatoes and chick peas

SERVES 4

15 ml/1 tbsp olive oil
1 onion, thinly sliced
1 garlic clove, finely chopped
2 carrots, thinly sliced
15 ml/1 tbsp grated fresh root ginger
2.5 ml/½ tsp ground cinnamon
2.5 ml/½ tsp ground turmeric
Salt and freshly ground black pepper
425 g/15 oz/large can of chick peas (garbanzos), drained

350 g/12 oz sweet potatoes, cut into cubes
450 ml/¾ pt/2 cups vegetable stock
Finely grated zest of 1 small lemon
2.5 ml/½ tsp dried mint
15 ml/1 tbsp lemon juice
300 g/11 oz packet of Quorn pieces, thawed if frozen

1 Preheat the slow cooker on High.

2 Heat the oil in a large pan and add the onion, garlic and carrots. Cook, stirring occasionally, until softened and beginning to brown.

3 Stir in the ginger, cinnamon, turmeric and seasoning. Add the chick peas, sweet potatoes, stock, lemon zest and mint.

4 Bring just to the boil, transfer to the slow cooker and stir gently.

5 Cover and cook on Low for 5–7 hours until tender, then stir in the lemon juice and Quorn and cook for a further 1 hour.

6 Serve hot.

SAVOURY
AND
SWEET
SAUCES

We all know that a sauce can transform plain ingredients into something really special. Here you will find a selection of savoury sauces that can be left to the gentle simmering of the slow cooker for several hours before being added to freshly cooked vegetables, rice or pasta (to name but a few).

I have also included some sweet sauces, which have shorter cooking times but are just as suitable for your slow cooker. Any one of them will turn a bowl of fruit or a scoop of ice cream into an elegant dessert or an indulgent pud!

This chunky, fresh-tasting tomato sauce is so easy to make and so full of flavour that any bought variety will pale into insignificance in comparison. It can be used in any number of ways, but is particularly good stirred through pasta, with freshly cooked vegetables.

chunky fresh two-tomato sauce

SERVES 6–8

15 ml/1 tbsp olive oil
1 onion, finely chopped
1 small carrot, finely chopped
1 celery stick, finely chopped
1 garlic clove, finely chopped
15 ml/1 tbsp plain (all-purpose) flour
300 ml/½ pt/1¼ cups vegetable stock

400 g/14 oz/large can of chopped tomatoes
15 ml/1 tbsp tomato purée (paste)
10 ml/2 tsp sugar
10 ml/2 tsp dried oregano
Salt and freshly ground black pepper
225 g/8 oz baby plum tomatoes

1 Preheat the slow cooker on High.

2 Heat the oil in a large pan, add the onion, carrot, celery and garlic and cook, stirring occasionally, until softened and just beginning to brown.

3 Stir in the flour, then gradually add the stock, stirring all the time. Add the canned tomatoes, tomato purée, sugar, oregano and seasoning.

4 Bring just to the boil, transfer to the slow cooker and stir gently.

5 Cover and cook on Low for 6–8 hours until the vegetables are very tender, then stir in the whole plum tomatoes and cook for a further 30 minutes.

6 Taste and adjust the seasoning before serving.

*This is great for serving with barbecued or grilled vegetables,
vegetable kebabs and vegetarian sausages and burgers, or for
brushing on before cooking. The recipe makes a larger quantity
of sauce than you might need for one meal, but any extra can be frozen.*

spicy-sweet
barbecue sauce

SERVES 8–10

30 ml/2 tbsp olive oil
2 onions, finely chopped
2 garlic cloves, finely chopped
90 ml/6 tbsp tomato ketchup (catsup)
60 ml/4 tbsp tomato purée (paste)
60 ml/4 tbsp Worcestershire sauce

30 ml/2 tbsp malt vinegar
30 ml/2 tbsp soft brown sugar
30 ml/2 tbsp made mustard, such as
   Dijon or wholegrain
Salt and freshly ground black pepper

1 Heat the oil in a large pan, add the onions and cook, stirring
occasionally, until softened but not browned.

2 Stir in the remaining ingredients and add 225 ml/8 fl oz/1 cup
of water.

3 Bring just to the boil, transfer to the slow cooker and stir gently.

4 Cover and cook on Low for 4–6 hours.

5 Stir well and taste and adjust the seasoning, if necessary, before
serving.

I love purple-skinned aubergines, and they combine here with the tomatoes and mushrooms to make a darkly coloured, rich-looking sauce. You could add a dash of red at Step 3 for a little extra luxury. It is delicious stirred into freshly cooked pasta.

aubergine and mushroom sauce

SERVES 4

45 ml/3 tbsp olive oil
1 onion, finely chopped
2 garlic cloves, finely chopped
1 aubergine (eggplant), cut into 1 cm/½ in cubes
100 g/4 oz chestnut mushrooms, thinly sliced

5 ml/1 tsp fennel seeds
450 ml/¾ pt/2 cups passata (sieved tomatoes)
5 ml/1 tsp sugar
5 ml/1 tsp dried oregano
Salt and freshly ground black pepper

1 Heat the oil in a large pan, add the onion and garlic and cook, stirring occasionally, until slightly softened.

2 Add the aubergine and mushrooms and cook, stirring occasionally, until softened and beginning to turn golden brown.

3 Stir in the fennel seeds, then add the remaining ingredients.

4 Bring just to the boil and transfer to the slow cooker.

5 Cover and cook on Low for 6–8 hours until the vegetables are very tender.

6 Stir well before serving.

During the long, slow cooking, this sauce develops a wonderfully mellow flavour. I often stir some cooked vegetables into it and spoon it over freshly cooked rice to make an easy but tempting meal. If you have any left over, it will freeze well.

red wine and chestnut mushroom sauce

SERVES 6–8

15 ml/1 tbsp olive oil
1 red onion, finely chopped
1 large garlic clove, finely chopped
100 g/4 oz chestnut mushrooms, thinly sliced
10 ml/2 tsp sugar

45 ml/3 tbsp plain (all-purpose) flour
300 ml/½ pt/1¼ cups red wine
300 ml½ pt/1¼ cups vegetable stock
30 ml/2 tbsp tomato purée (paste)
Salt and freshly ground black pepper

1 Heat the oil in a pan and add the onion, garlic, mushrooms and sugar. Cook, stirring occasionally, until softened but not browned.

2 Add the flour and cook, stirring, for 1 minute.

3 Remove from the heat and gradually stir in the wine and stock. Add the tomato purée and a little seasoning.

4 Bring just to the boil, stirring, and then transfer to the slow cooker.

5 Cover and cook on Low for 6–8 hours until the vegetables are very soft.

6 Stir well and taste and adjust the seasoning, if necessary, before serving.

Roasted, grilled or barbecued vegetable dishes are often very good served just as they are, but many would be transformed with a serving of this refreshingly minty curry sauce on the side. Serve with some freshly cooked basmati or long-grain rice.

curry sauce with tomato, apple and mint

SERVES 6–8

15 ml/1 tbsp olive oil
3 onions, finely chopped
10 ml/2 tsp sugar
30 ml/2 tbsp medium curry paste
45 ml/3 tbsp plain (all-purpose) flour
600 ml/1 pt/2½ cups vegetable stock
225 g/8 oz/small can of chopped tomatoes

30 ml/2 tbsp lemon juice
30 ml/2 tbsp mango chutney, large pieces finely chopped
1 crisp eating (dessert) apple
30–45 ml/2–3 tbsp chopped fresh mint
Salt and freshly ground black pepper

1 Heat the oil in a large pan, add the onions and sugar and cook, stirring occasionally, until soft and golden brown.

2 Add the curry paste and cook, stirring, for 1–2 minutes.

3 Stir in the flour, then gradually stir in the stock. Add the tomatoes, lemon juice and chutney.

4 Bring just to the boil, stirring all the time, and transfer to the slow cooker.

5 Cover and cook on Low for about 6–8 hours until the onions are very tender.

6 Peel and core the apple and cut into small dice. Stir into the sauce with the mint and add seasoning to taste.

7 Cover and cook for 30 minutes or until the apple is soft.

8 Stir well before serving.

Cranberry sauce is, of course, the traditional accompaniment to roast turkey but there is no reason why you can't enjoy it with a variety of meatless dishes. Fresh cranberries give the best flavour.

cranberry sauce

SERVES 6

225 g/8 oz fresh or thawed frozen cranberries
300 ml/½ pt/1¼ cups orange juice

175–225g/6–8 oz caster (superfine) sugar

1   Put the cranberries into the slow cooker and stir in the orange juice.

2   Cover and cook on High for 2–3 hours or until the cranberries have popped open.

3   Stir in the sugar until dissolved.

4   Continue to cook on High for 1 hour, stirring once or twice, until the sauce has thickened slightly.

This sauce is lovely served either hot or chilled with ice-cream, fruit or cake. It is delicious on muesli for breakfast, too. It's a wonderful way to use home-grown fruit in season, and you can use one type or try a mixture.

soft fruit sauce

MAKES ABOUT 600 ML/1 PT/2½ CUPS

500 g/18 oz/2¼ cups prepared soft fruit, such as raspberries, blackberries, strawberries, blueberries or currants
30 ml/2 tbsp lemon juice

60 ml/4 tbsp caster (superfine) sugar
30 ml/2 tbsp orange or blackcurrant liqueur

1   Put the fruit in the slow cooker in an even layer, then sprinkle the lemon juice and sugar over the fruit.

2   Cover and cook on Low for 2–3½ hours.

3   Gently stir in the liqueur just before serving.

This must be everyone's favourite sweet sauce! It's especially good with bananas and chocolate desserts and trickled over plain vanilla ice-cream. The small quantity of lemon juice gives a pleasant hint of sharpness.

butterscotch sauce

SERVES 4–6

50 g/2 oz/¼ cup butter or margarine
50 g/2 oz/¼ cup soft brown sugar
175 g/6 oz/¾ cup golden (light corn) syrup

10 ml/2 tsp lemon juice
150 ml/¼ pt/⅔ cup double (heavy) cream

1 Put all the ingredients into an ovenproof dish and cover securely with foil.

2 Put the dish into the slow cooker and pour in enough cold water to come halfway up the sides of the dish.

3 Cover and cook on Low for 3–4 hours.

4 Stir well before serving.

The rich coffee and chocolate flavour of this dessert sauce dresses up plain cake to perfection and goes so well with ice-cream and poached fruit. The quantity of sugar will depend on the amount of cocoa solids in the chocolate.

mocha fudge sauce

SERVES 6–8

410 g/14 oz/large can of evaporated milk
225 g/8 oz bar of plain (semi-sweet) chocolate

About 45 ml/3 tbsp light muscovado sugar
30 ml/2 tbsp coffee essence (extract)

1 Lightly whisk the milk until smooth. Pour into the slow cooker.

2 Break the chocolate into squares and add to the milk.

3 Stir in the sugar and coffee essence.

4 Cover and cook on Low for 2–3 hours, stirring after 1 hour, until the sauce is smooth, thick and shiny.

If you can resist the temptation to devour this sauce just as it is, pour it over cooked or fresh ripe pears, ice-cream or desserts such as profiteroles. Alternatively, use it as a fondue, with chunks of fruit and cake speared on sticks for dipping.

creamy dark chocolate sauce with liqueur

SERVES 6–8

350 g/12 oz plain (semi-sweet) chocolate
300 ml/½ pt/1¼ cups double (heavy) cream

30 ml/2 tbsp golden (light corn) or maple syrup
5 ml/1 tsp finely grated orange zest
60 ml/4 tbsp rum, brandy or orange liqueur

1   Break the chocolate into the slow cooker and heat on High for about 30–40 minutes until melted.

2   Stir in the cream, syrup and orange zest.

3   Cover and cook on Low for 1–2 hours, stirring after 1 hour, until the sauce is smooth and thick.

4   Just before serving, stir in the rum, brandy or liqueur.

PUDDINGS
AND
DESSERTS

Mine is a family of pudding lovers. And whether it's a bowl of delicate fruit that retains its beautiful shape, a creamy brûlée, a rice pudding or a good old-fashioned steamed pud, the slow cooker does them all to perfection.

If you have never cooked (and reheated) your Christmas pudding in a slow cooker, I urge you to try it – see page 122. The feeling of smug satisfaction on Christmas day, knowing that the pudding is taking care of itself, gently reheating in the corner of your kitchen, will be a gift to yourself!

You can buy ras el hanout, *an exotic spice blend, in most supermarkets and delicatessens. Its flavour complements the rhubarb in this recipe beautifully. It can be served warm or chilled, just as it is or with a dollop of thick Greek-style yoghurt and some crisp biscuits.*

sweet rhubarb
with moroccan spices

SERVES 4

75 g/3 oz/⅓ cup golden caster
   (superfine) sugar
5 ml/1 tsp ras el hanout

450 g/1 lb prepared rhubarb, cut into
   2.5 cm/1 in lengths
45 ml/3 tbsp fresh orange juice

1 Combine the sugar and spice mix and toss the rhubarb in it.

2 Transfer to the slow cooker.

3 Stir in the orange juice and spread the rhubarb in an even layer.

4 Cover and cook on Low for 2–3½ hours until the rhubarb is tender but still holding its shape.

This works well with under-ripe peaches. If you like, when the peaches are cooked pour off the juice into a saucepan and boil rapidly to reduce it, then add the rose water and almond essence and pour over the peaches before leaving to cool. Serve chilled with crisp biscuits and whipped cream.

peaches in rose water and almond syrup

SERVES 6

6 small firm peaches
90 ml/6 tbsp golden caster
   (superfine) sugar
A few strips of lemon zest

Juice of ½ lemon
30 ml/2 tbsp rose water
1.5 ml/¼ tsp almond essence
   (extract)

1   Pour sufficient boiling water over the peaches to cover them. Leave to stand for a few minutes before draining, after which you should be able to peel off the skins easily. Once peeled, cut them in half and remove the stones (pits).

2   Put the peach halves into the slow cooker in an even layer, cut side down. Pour over 600 ml/1 pt/2½ cups of boiling water. Sprinkle the sugar over and add the lemon zest and juice.

3   Cover and cook on High for 3–5 hours until the peaches are soft and tender.

4   Gently stir in the rose water and almond essence.

5   Cover and leave to cool, then chill until required.

These delicious creamy, fruity desserts are also good made using
other ripe summer fruits such as raspberries, strawberries,
cherries or nectarines, or even sliced bananas. Make sure you have four
ramekins that will fit easily in your slow cooker.

fresh mango
creamy crèmes brûlées

SERVES 4

4 egg yolks
2.5 ml/½ tsp vanilla essence (extract)
75 g/3 oz/⅓ cup caster (superfine)
 sugar

300 ml/½ pt/1¼ cups double (heavy)
 cream
150 ml/¼ pt/⅔ cup milk
1 ripe mango, peeled, stoned (pitted)
 and chopped

1 Preheat the slow cooker on High.

2 Lightly whisk together the egg yolks, vanilla essence and 45 ml/3 tbsp of the sugar.

3 Heat the cream and milk gently in a pan on the hob (or in a jug in the microwave) until hot but not boiling. Pour on to the egg mixture, stirring continuously with the whisk.

4 Spoon the mango pieces into the base of four individual ovenproof ramekins (custard cups) and strain the custard over the top.

5 Put the dishes, side by side, in the slow cooker and pour in sufficient boiling water to come halfway up their sides.

6 Cover and cook on Low for 3–4½ hours or until set.

7 Lift out, leave to cool, then chill for several hours.

8 Sprinkle the remaining sugar evenly over the top of the custards and put under a hot grill (broiler) for 2–3 minutes until the sugar turns to caramel.

9 Leave to cool, then chill until required.

Much of the moist sweetness of this pudding comes from the grated carrot. It is delicious served with custard, ice-cream or one of the dessert sauces in this book. Or you could make a simple sauce by heating golden or maple syrup with a little fresh orange juice.

passion cake pudding with carrot and walnuts

SERVES 4–6

100 g/4 oz/½ cup softened butter or margarine, plus extra for greasing
100 g/4 oz/½ cup golden caster (superfine) sugar
2 eggs, lightly beaten
100 g/4 oz/⅔ cup finely grated carrot
Finely grated zest and juice of 1 orange
100 g/4 oz/1 cup self-raising (self-rising) flour
1.5 ml/¼ tsp baking powder
45 ml/3 tbsp finely chopped walnuts
30 ml/2 tbsp sultanas (golden raisins)

1 Preheat the slow cooker on High.

2 Lightly grease a 900 ml/1½ pt/3¾ cup pudding basin.

3 Beat the butter or margarine with the sugar until light and fluffy. Gradually beat in the eggs, then the carrot and orange zest. Sift the flour and baking powder over the top and fold in gently. Stir in 30 ml/2 tbsp of the orange juice and the walnuts and sultanas.

4 Spoon the mixture into the prepared basin, cover securely with greased foil and put into the slow cooker.

5 Cover and cook on High for 3½–4½ hours until cooked and firm to the touch.

6 Turn out on to a warmed plate to serve.

I love maple syrup with walnuts – it's a combination made in heaven!
However, if you don't have maple syrup to hand, ordinary golden
syrup will work just as well. Whipped cream is good served with this
dessert, but plain Greek-style yoghurt is even better.

hot walnut and
maple syrup pudding

SERVES 4–6

100 g/4 oz/½ cup softened butter or
   margarine, plus extra for greasing
60 ml/4 tbsp syrup
60 ml/4 tbsp roughly chopped
   walnuts

100 g/4 oz/½ cup golden caster
   (superfine) sugar
2 eggs, lightly beaten
175 g/6 oz/1½ cups self-raising (self-
   rising) flour
30 ml/2 tbsp milk

1 Preheat the slow cooker on High.

2 Lightly grease a 1.2 litre/2 pt/5 cup pudding basin. Spoon the
syrup into it and sprinkle 30 ml/2 tbsp of the walnuts on top.

3 Beat the butter or margarine with the sugar until light and fluffy.
Gradually beat in the eggs. Sift the flour over the top and fold in
gently. Stir in the milk and the remaining walnuts.

4 Spoon the mixture into the prepared basin, cover securely with
greased foil and put into the slow cooker.

5 Cover and cook on High for 3½–4½ hours until cooked and firm to
the touch.

6 Turn out on to a warmed plate to serve.

You could use ordinary soft light brown sugar in this recipe but, if you can, do use light muscovado. Its delicate, fudge-like flavour is perfect with the citrus tang of lemon and lime. The finished pudding should have a rather crumbly texture. Serve with custard.

crumbly lemon and lime oat pudding

SERVES 4–6

75 g/3 oz/⅓ cup softened butter or margarine, plus extra for greasing
100 g/4 oz/½ cup light muscovado sugar
Finely grated zest of 1 lemon
Finely grated zest of 1 lime
1 large egg, lightly beaten

50 g/2 oz/½ cup self-raising (self-rising) flour
2.5 ml/½ tsp baking powder
50 g/2 oz/½ cup rolled oats
About 45 ml/3 tbsp lemon or lime juice, or a mixture of both

1 Preheat the slow cooker on High.

2 Lightly grease a 600 ml/1 pt/2½ cup pudding basin and put a small circle of non-stick baking parchment in the bottom.

3 Beat the butter or margarine with the sugar and citrus zests until light and fluffy. Gradually beat in the egg. Sift the flour and baking powder over the top and add the oats. Gently fold in, adding enough juice to make a soft consistency that drops off the spoon.

4 Spoon the mixture into the prepared basin, cover securely with greased foil and put into the slow cooker. Pour in sufficient hot water to come halfway up the sides of the basin.

5 Cover and cook on High for 3–4 hours until cooked through.

6 Turn out on to a warmed plate to serve.

This must be the ultimate sweet pudding. Try soaking the dates in strong tea (Earl Grey is especially good) instead of water. There is a recipe for butterscotch sauce in this book, but I thought I'd include this one, as your slow cooker will already be busy making the pudding!

sticky toffee pudding
with butterscotch sauce

SERVES 6–8

175 g/6 oz/1 cup chopped stoned (pitted) dates
75 g/3 oz/¾ cup softened butter or margarine, plus extra for greasing
100 g/4 oz/½ cup dark muscovado sugar
5 ml/1 tsp vanilla essence (extract)
2 eggs, lightly beaten
150 g/5 oz/1 cup plain (all-purpose) flour

7.5 ml/1½ tsp baking powder

FOR THE SAUCE
50 g/2 oz/¼ cup butter or margarine
100 g/4 oz/½ cup dark muscovado sugar
150 ml/¼ pt/⅔ cup double (heavy) cream
Toasted flaked (slivered) almonds, to garnish

1 Put the dates into a small bowl, pour over 120 ml/4 fl oz/½ cup of boiling water and leave to cool completely.

2 Preheat the slow cooker on High. Lightly grease a 15–18 cm/ 6–7 in ovenproof soufflé dish and line the base with non-stick baking parchment.

3 Beat the softened butter or margarine with the sugar and vanilla essence until light and fluffy. Gradually beat in the eggs. Sift the flour and baking powder over the top and add the dates and any liquid. Fold in.

4 Spoon the mixture into the prepared dish and level the surface. Cover securely with greased foil and put into the slow cooker. Pour in sufficient hot water to come halfway up the sides of the dish.

5 Cover and cook on High for 3½–4½ hours until cooked through and firm to the touch.

6 Just before serving, make the sauce. Put the butter or margarine, sugar and cream into a small pan on the hob or into a ju in the microwave and heat, stirring occasionally, until the fat h melted and the sugar has dissolved. Bring to the boil and allow bubble gently for 1–2 minutes.

7 Turn the pudding out gently on to a warmed plate. Slice serve with the sauce spooned over and topped with a few toast ts.

This creamy pudding is lightly scented with nutmeg, and the ora. flower water adds the wonderful perfume of bitter-orange blosson Leave it out if you want to make a more traditional-style rice pud. The longer it is in the slow cooker, the thicker it will become.

scented rice pudding

SERVES 6

A little butter or margarine, for greasing
75 g/3 oz/⅓ cup round-grain (pudding) rice, rinsed
900 ml/1½ pts/3¾ cups milk

45 ml/3 tbsp caster (superfine
2.5 ml/½ tsp vanilla essence (e
Freshly grated nutmeg
60 ml/4 tbsp double (heavy) cr
30 ml/2 tbsp orange flower wat

1 Grease the inside of the slow cooker.

2 Put the rice into the slow cooker and stir in the milk, sugar and vanilla essence. Grate a little nutmeg over the top.

3 Cover and cook on Low for 6–9 hours, depending on how thick you want it, stirring once or twice during the final 2 hours if possible.

4 About 15 minutes before serving, stir in the cream.

5 Stir in the orange flower water immediately before serving. It is delicious hot or warm.

A lovely moist dessert that gives a great excuse to take a day off in autumn to go blackberry-picking. But it works equally well with blueberries, raspberries, apricot halves or quartered plums. Serve with custard, pouring cream or crème fraîche.

sponge pudding with blueberry and muscovado topping

SERVES 6

FOR THE TOPPING
25 g/1 oz/2 tbsp butter or margarine, plus extra for greasing
30 ml/2 tbsp light muscovado sugar
225 g/8 oz fresh blueberries

FOR THE SPONGE
100 g/4 oz/½ cup softened butter or margarine
100 g/4 oz/½ cup light muscovado sugar
2 eggs, lightly beaten
30 ml/2 tbsp milk
100 g/4 oz/1 cup self-raising (self-rising) flour
2.5 ml/½ tsp baking powder
5 ml/1 tsp ground cinnamon

1 Preheat the slow cooker on High.

2 First, make the topping. Lightly grease the sides of a 15–18 cm/ 6–7 in ovenproof soufflé dish. Melt the butter or margarine and pour into the dish, swirling it so that it covers the base. Sprinkle the sugar over and top with the blueberries.

3 Put all the sponge ingredients into a mixing bowl and beat well for 2–3 minutes until smooth and fluffy.

4 Spoon the mixture over the blueberries and level the surface. Cover securely with greased foil and put into the slow cooker. Pour in sufficient hot water to come halfway up the sides of the dish.

5 Cover and cook on High for 2½–3½ hours until cooked through and firm to the touch.

6 Turn the pudding out gently on to a warmed plate to serve.

A creamy rice pudding made delightfully fragrant with cardamom, cinnamon and cloves. It is a version of the Indian rice dessert khir. *The rose water is sprinkled on top of the finished pudding to add an extra soft, sweet flavour.*

spiced indian rice pudding with raisins and almonds

SERVES 6

A little butter or margarine, for greasing
50 g/2 oz/¼ cup round-grain (pudding) rice, rinsed
900 ml/1½ pts/3¾ cups milk
150 ml/¼ pt/⅔ cup double (heavy) cream
45 ml/3 tbsp golden caster (superfine) or soft brown sugar

1 cinnamon stick
2 whole cloves
Seeds from 4 cardamom pods
30 ml/2 tbsp raisins or sultanas (golden raisins)
30 ml/2 tbsp flaked (slivered) almonds
A little rose water

1 Grease the inside of the slow cooker.

2 Put the rice into the slow cooker and stir in all the ingredients except the rose water.

3 Cover and cook on Low for 6–8 hours, until thick and creamy, stirring once or twice during the final 2 hours if possible.

4 Transfer to a serving dish and leave until cool. Chill for several hours or until required.

5 Just before serving, sprinkle the top of the pudding with rose water.

Serve this hot or chilled, as a dessert with whipped cream, yoghurt or ice-cream, or use it in the morning to jazz up your breakfast muesli. You can ring the changes almost endlessly by using different varieties of fruit infusion bag. Slow cooking will make the dried fruit moist and tender.

cooked fruit and almond salad with honey

SERVES 6

250 g/9 oz/large packet of mixed
   dried fruit salad
2 fruit infusion bags

30 ml/2 tbsp clear honey
30 ml/2 tbsp toasted flaked (slivered)
   almonds

1   Put the fruit and the infusion bags into the slow cooker and pour over 750 ml/1¼ pts/3 cups of boiling water. Stir in the honey.

2   Cover and cook on Low for 8–10 hours until the fruit is plumped up and soft.

3   Remove the infusion bags, squeezing them to extract every last drop of flavour.

4   Stir in the almonds, then serve hot. Alternatively, cool and chill until required and serve cold.

This takes a little time to prepare and arrange in the dish, but rest assured the result will be worth the effort! For a change, try replacing the marmalade with your favourite conserve or with chocolate or hazelnut spread. Serve the pudding with pouring cream or vanilla ice-cream.

sultana and orange bread and butter pudding

SERVES 4–6

A little butter or margarine, for greasing and spreading
6 slices of bread
Marmalade, for spreading
45 ml/3 tbsp sultanas (golden raisins)
2 large eggs
5 ml/1 tsp vanilla essence (extract)
40 g/1½ oz/⅓ cup caster (superfine) sugar
450 ml/¾ pt/2 cups milk
150 ml/¼ pt/⅔ cup double (heavy) cream

1 Lightly grease a deep dish that will fit into the slow cooker (a soufflé dish is ideal). Butter the slices of bread on one side, spread thinly with marmalade, make into sandwiches and cut into quarters. Arrange the bread, overlapping, in the prepared dish, distributing the sultanas between and over them.

2 Beat the eggs with the vanilla essence and sugar. Heat the milk and cream on the hob or in the microwave until hot but not boiling and gradually mix it into the eggs. Strain the mixture over the slices of bread.

3 Put into the slow cooker and pour in sufficient boiling water to come halfway up the sides of the dish.

4 Cover and cook on High for 1½–2 hours until the bread is puffed up and the egg custard has set.

5 Lift out of the slow cooker and leave to stand for 5–10 minutes, during which time the bread will fall back into the dish, and then serve.

This must be one of the most wickedly indulgent puddings ever! Serve each one with a piece of the lemon – this balances the richness of the sauce. I like to serve it with thick plain yoghurt. If your lemon isn't unwaxed, give it a good scrub under hot water to remove the thin wax coating.

rich lemon pond pudding with muscovado

SERVES 6

175 g/6 oz/1½ cups self-raising (self-rising) flour
75 g/3 oz/¾ cup chopped (shredded) vegetable suet
175 g/6 oz/¾ cup butter, cut into small cubes, plus extra for greasing

175 g/6 oz/¾ cup light muscovado sugar
1 large unwaxed lemon
30 ml/2 tbsp raisins

1   Sift the flour into a mixing bowl and stir in the suet. Using a round-bladed knife, stir in sufficient cold water to make a soft dough. Knead lightly until smooth.

2   On a lightly floured surface, roll out the dough into a circle about 32 cm/13 in in diameter. Cut out one quarter of the dough in a wedge, and reserve.

3   Lightly grease a 1.2 litre/2 pt/5 cup pudding basin and line it with the large piece of dough, pinching the edges together to seal the seam.

4   Put half the butter and half the sugar into the lined basin.

5   With a skewer, pierce the lemon all over. Gently push the lemon into the butter and sugar mixture. Add the raisins, then scatter the remaining butter and sugar over and around the lemon.

6   Roll out the reserved dough to form a lid, place on top and pinch the edges together to seal them well. Cover securely with greased foil and put into the slow cooker. Pour in sufficient hot water to come halfway up the sides of the dish.

7   Cover and cook on High for 5½–7 hours.

8   Turn the pudding out gently on to a warmed plate and serve immediately.

Ginger and lemongrass both enhance the delicate flavour of pears, though elderflower cordial would work well too or, to give the pears extra colour, try cranberry and orange. Serve the pears chilled with their syrup spooned over and a dollop of thick cream.

pears in ginger and lemongrass syrup

SERVES 6

6 whole cloves
1 cinnamon stick
150 ml/¼ pt/⅔ cup ginger and
   lemongrass cordial

30 ml/2 tbsp clear honey
6 firm pears, peeled and left whole

1 Put the cloves, cinnamon, cordial and honey into the slow cooker. Add the pears, laying them on their sides.

2 Pour over just enough boiling water to cover the pears.

3 Cover and cook on Low for 6–10 hours until the pears are very soft.

4 With a draining spoon, carefully transfer the pears to a serving dish.

5 Pour the juices with the spices into a large pan. Bring to the boil and bubble until the mixture has reduced by about two-thirds or to your required consistency (check it by tasting – it should be sweet with a good strong flavour).

6 Strain the syrup over the pears and leave to cool completely.

7 Chill until required.

I just had to include this recipe. Christmas pudding is ideal for slow cooking – just pop it in to cook all day or overnight. When it comes to reheating the pud on Christmas day, it can be left to its own devices in the slow cooker, away from the hustle and bustle.

christmas pudding

SERVES 8

50 g/2 oz/½ cup plain (all-purpose) flour
5 ml/1 tsp ground mixed (apple-pie) spice
100 g/4 oz/2 cups fresh white breadcrumbs
140 g/5 oz/1¼ cups chopped (shredded) vegetable suet
100 g/4 oz/½ cup soft brown sugar
400 g/14 oz/3 cups dried mixed fruit (fruit cake mix)

50 g/2 oz/½ cup blanched and chopped almonds
1 small carrot, finely grated
Finely grated zest and juice of 1 orange
2 eggs, beaten
15 ml/1 tbsp black treacle (molasses)
15 ml/1 tbsp brandy or dry sherry
75 ml/5 tbsp beer or milk
A little butter or margarine, for greasing

1 Preheat the slow cooker on High while you make the pudding.

2 Sift the flour and spice into a large bowl and mix in the breadcrumbs, suet, sugar, fruit, nuts, carrot and orange zest.

3 Whisk together the orange juice, eggs, treacle, brandy or sherry and beer or milk. Add to the bowl and mix well.

4 Spoon the mixture into a greased 1.2 litre/2 pt/5 cup pudding basin and level the top. Cover securely with greased foil.

5 Stand the basin in the slow cooker and pour in sufficient water to come three-quarters of the way up the sides of the basin.

6 Cover and cook on High for 10–12 hours.

7 Remove from the slow cooker, leave to cool completely, wrap in more foil and store in a cool, dark place.

8 To reheat before serving, preheat the slow cooker on High for 20 minutes. Stand the pudding in the slow cooker and pour in sufficient water to come three-quarters of the way up the sides of the basin. Cover and cook on Low for about 8 hours, or on High for about 4 hours.

This is a dessert that is just bursting with the warmth and exotic flavours of the Caribbean, though for convenience I use canned mango because the syrup gives the right texture and moistness. This pudding is cooked and served straight from the crock pot.

mango, banana and coconut pudding

SERVES 6

100 g/4 oz/½ cup softened butter or margarine, plus extra for greasing
410 g/14 oz/large can of mango slices in syrup
2 bananas
100 g/4 oz/½ cup caster (superfine) sugar

175 g/6 oz/1½ cups self-raising (self-rising) flour
2.5 ml/½ tsp baking powder
2 large eggs, lightly beaten
30 ml/2 tbsp desiccated (shredded) coconut

1 Lightly grease the inside of the slow cooker pot. Drain the mango, reserving the syrup, and arrange the slices evenly in the slow cooker. Slice the bananas over the top and drizzle with 45 ml/ 3 tbsp of the reserved syrup.

2 Preheat the slow cooker on High while you prepare the pudding mixture.

3 Put the remaining ingredients into a mixing bowl and add 60 ml/ 4 tbsp of the reserved syrup. Beat well for 2–3 minutes until smooth and fluffy.

4 Spoon the pudding mixture evenly over the top of the fruit and level the surface.

5 Cover and cook on High for 2½–3½ hours until the pudding is firm to the touch.

A great pudding to make when your apple tree is providing ample fruit and you want a change from the usual crumbles and pies. The cooking time will depend on the size of the apples – make sure they will fit snugly inside your slow cooker. Serve with custard.

spiced apples
with fruit and almonds

SERVES 4

4 Bramley cooking (tart) apples
60 ml/4 tbsp chopped dried fruit, such as pears, apricots, figs or dates
25 g/1 oz/¼ cup almonds, finely chopped

1.5 ml/¼ tsp ground cinnamon
1.5 ml/¼ tsp finely grated nutmeg
60 ml/4 tbsp light muscovado sugar
25 g/1 oz/2 tbsp butter (optional)
60 ml/4 tbsp orange juice

1 Core the apples and peel off a thin strip around the centre of each (like the equator!). Put them into the slow cooker.

2 Mix the dried fruit with the almonds, cinnamon, nutmeg and sugar. Spoon the mixture into the apples, pressing it in and piling any excess on top.

3 Top each apple with one quarter of the butter (if using) and pour the orange juice around them.

4 Cover and cook on Low for 4–6 hours until the apples are tender.

CAKES

Many people are surprised at how versatile a slow cooker can be. I have discovered that cakes cooked in this way are amazingly successful, and even the ones that fail to turn out as I expected are usually delicious served as a pudding!

I usually cook cakes without a cover (but with the lid of the slow cooker in place) but if you find that the surface of the cooked cake turns out too moist, you may prefer to cover the dish with a 'hat' of baking parchment. Always preheat the slow cooker while you are mixing the ingredients, and always cook cakes on High.

This is an interesting variation on the ever-popular gingerbread, which you could also easily make just by replacing the coriander with ground ginger. The icing is an optional extra – it makes an attractive finish but the cake is just as good eaten plain.

orange and coriander cake with orange icing

MAKES AN 18 CM/7 IN CAKE

100 g/4 oz/½ cup butter or margarine, plus extra for greasing
350 g/12 oz/3 cups plain (all-purpose) flour
A pinch of salt
15 ml/1 tbsp ground coriander
10 ml/2 tsp baking powder
2.5 ml/½ tsp bicarbonate of soda (baking soda)
175 g/6 oz/¾ cup soft brown sugar

225 g/8 oz/⅔ cup golden (light corn) syrup
1 egg, lightly beaten
Finely grated zest of 1 orange
200 ml/7 fl oz/scant 1 cup milk
For the icing (frosting)
100 g/4 oz/⅔ cup icing (confectioners') sugar
15 ml/1 tbsp orange juice

1 Preheat the slow cooker on High.

2 Lightly grease and line the base of an 18 cm/7 in cake tin (pan) or ovenproof dish with non-stick baking parchment.

3 Sift the flour, salt, coriander, baking powder and bicarbonate of soda into a mixing bowl.

4 Put the sugar, butter or margarine and syrup into a small pan or in a bowl in the microwave and heat gently, stirring occasionally, until just melted. Remove from the heat.

5 Whisk the egg and orange zest into the milk. Add the milk and syrup mixtures to the flour and beat well until smooth. Pour into the prepared tin.

6 Put into the slow cooker and pour in sufficient hot water to come halfway up the sides of the tin.

7 Cover and cook on High for 5–7 hours until cooked through and firm to the touch.

8 Lift out of the slow cooker and allow to stand for 10 minutes. Loosen the sides with a knife, turn out on to a wire rack lined with non-stick baking parchment, and leave to cool completely.

9 Meanwhile, make the icing, if using. Mix sufficient icing sugar with orange juice to make a thin pouring consistency. Drizzle over the top and sides of the cooled cake.

Date and walnut cake is a classic, and a favourite in many families
– but I bet you never thought it could be made in a slow cooker.
Serve thick slices of this coffee break or teatime treat
with a good dollop of Greek-style yoghurt or crème fraîche.

date and walnut cake
with muscovado and nutmeg

MAKES AN 18 CM/7 IN CAKE

100 g/4 oz/½ cup butter or margarine,
plus extra for greasing
225 g/8 oz/2 cups plain (all-purpose)
flour
10 ml/2 tsp baking powder
2.5 ml/½ tsp grated nutmeg

100 g/4 oz/⅔ cup ready-to-eat dried
dates, chopped
40 g/1½ oz/⅓ cup chopped walnuts
100 g/4 oz/¾ cup dark muscovado
sugar
2 eggs
About 150 ml/¼ pt/⅔ cup milk

1 Preheat the slow cooker on High.

2 Lightly grease and line the base of an 18 cm/7 in ovenproof soufflé dish with non-stick baking parchment.

3 Sift the flour, baking powder and nutmeg into a mixing bowl and, using your fingertips, rub in the butter or margarine until the mixture resembles fine breadcrumbs. (This can also be done in a food processor.)

4 Stir in the dates, walnuts and sugar.

5 Lightly whisk the eggs into the milk and stir into the dry ingredients. Spoon the mixture into the prepared dish and level the surface.

6 Put into the slow cooker and pour in sufficient hot water to come halfway up the sides of the dish.

7 Cover and cook on High for 4–6 hours until cooked through and firm to the touch.

8 Lift out of the slow cooker and allow to stand for 10 minutes. Loosen the sides with a knife, turn out on to a wire rack lined with non-stick baking parchment and leave to cool completely.

This is a slow cooked version of another popular teatime speciality. Drizzle the icing over the cake while it is still warm, so some seeps into the sponge, making it even moister and more lemony, and the rest stays on top, setting as it cools to a lovely, slightly crunchy topping.

lemon drizzle cake with crunchy lemon glaze

MAKES AN 18 CM/7 IN CAKE

100 g/4 oz/½ cup softened butter or margarine, plus extra for greasing
175 g/6 oz/¾ cup caster (superfine) sugar
175 g/6 oz/1½ cups self-raising (self-rising) flour
2 eggs
30 ml/2 tbsp milk
Finely grated zest of 1 lemon
15 ml/1 tbsp lemon juice
For the icing (frosting)
30 ml/2 tbsp lemon juice
150 g/5 oz/scant 1 cup tbsp icing (confectioners') sugar

1 Preheat the slow cooker on High.

2 Lightly grease and line the base of an 18 cm/7 in ovenproof soufflé dish with non-stick baking parchment.

3 Put the butter or margarine into a mixing bowl with the sugar, flour, eggs, milk, lemon zest and juice. Beat until smooth, then spoon the mixture into the prepared dish and level the surface.

4 Put into the slow cooker and pour in sufficient hot water to come halfway up the sides of the dish.

5 Cover and cook on High for 2–3 hours until cooked through and firm to the touch.

6 Lift out of the slow cooker and allow to stand for 5 minutes before loosening the sides with a knife.

7 Carefully insert a fine skewer in several places into the top of the cake.

8 Mix the ingredients for the icing, blending until smooth, and slowly spoon or pour the mixture over the top of the cake.

9 Leave the cake to cool in the dish before turning out and serving.

The combination of ground almonds and semolina, rather than ordinary flour, produces a cake with a very pleasing texture. As well as being a delicious cake, it can also be served while still hot as a pudding – it is delicious with Greek-style yoghurt.

almond cake
with lemon and honey topping

MAKES AN 18 CM/7 IN CAKE

100 g/4 oz/½ cup softened butter or margarine, plus extra for greasing
75 g/3 oz/⅓ cup caster (superfine) sugar
100 g/4 oz/½ cup semolina (cream of wheat)
75 g/3 oz/¾ cup ground almonds

2 eggs
Finely grated zest of 1 lemon
60 ml/4 tbsp lemon juice

FOR THE TOPPING
60 ml/4 tbsp lemon juice
60 ml/4 tbsp clear honey

1 Preheat the slow cooker on High.

2 Lightly grease and line the base of an 18 cm/7 in ovenproof soufflé dish with non-stick baking parchment.

3 Put the butter or margarine into a mixing bowl and add the remaining ingredients. Beat well until smooth.

4 Spoon the mixture into the prepared dish and level the surface.

5 Put into the slow cooker and pour in sufficient hot water to come halfway up the sides of the dish.

6 Cover and cook on High for 2½–3 hours until cooked through and firm to the touch.

7 Lift out of the slow cooker and allow to stand for 5 minutes, then loosen the sides with a knife and turn the cake out on to a wire rack lined with non-stick baking parchment.

8 Stir together the lemon juice and honey – this may be easier if you heat it – and spoon it slowly over the top of the cake until it has all been absorbed.

9 Serve warm or cold.

Cherries and coconut – another of those combinations that work so well! The idea with this impressive cake is that the cherries remain perched on top to give a decorative finish, so you will have to turn it out on to the wire rack very carefully.

glacé cherry and coconut cake

MAKES AN 18 CM/7 IN CAKE

100 g/4 oz/½ cup butter or margarine, plus extra for greasing
225 g/8 oz/2 cups self-raising (self-rising) flour
100 g/4 oz/½ cup caster (superfine) sugar
75 g/3 oz/¾ cup desiccated (shredded) coconut

100 g/4 oz/½ cup glacé (candied) cherries, finely chopped
2 eggs
1.5 ml/¼ tsp almond essence (extract)
150 ml/¼ pt/⅔ cup milk
A few whole glacé cherries, for decoration

1 Preheat the slow cooker on High.

2 Lightly grease and line the base of an 18 cm/7 in ovenproof soufflé dish with non-stick baking parchment.

3 Sift the flour into a mixing bowl and, using your fingertips, rub in the butter or margarine until the mixture resembles fine breadcrumbs. (This can be done in a food processor.)

4 Stir in the sugar, coconut and chopped cherries.

5 Lightly whisk the eggs and almond essence into the milk and stir into the dry ingredients.

6 Spoon the mixture into the prepared dish and level the surface. Cut the whole cherries in half and arrange on top.

7 Put into the slow cooker and pour in sufficient hot water to come halfway up the sides of the dish.

8 Cover and cook on High for 2½–3 hours until cooked through and firm to the touch.

9 Lift out of the slow cooker and allow to stand for 10 minutes, then loosen the sides with a knife, turn out on to a wire rack and leave to cool completely before serving.

This is a cross between a cake and a pudding – so you could serve it as either. It's wonderfully gooey and rich so you won't need to serve very big slices. Think about making it for an older child's birthday party – I'm sure it would go down very well indeed!

rich peanut butter cake
with chocolate chips

MAKES AN 18 CM/7 IN CAKE

100 g/4 oz/½ cup butter or margarine, plus extra for greasing
225 g/8 oz/2 cups plain (all-purpose) flour
10 ml/2 tsp baking powder
100 g/4 oz/½ cup caster (superfine) sugar

2 eggs
150 ml/¼ pt/small carton of soured (dairy sour) cream
30 ml/2 tbsp milk
45 ml/3 tbsp peanut butter
5 ml/1 tsp vanilla essence (extract)
85 g/3 oz/½ cup chocolate chips

1 Preheat the slow cooker on High.

2 Lightly grease and line the base of an 18 cm/7 in ovenproof soufflé dish with non-stick baking parchment.

3 Sift the flour and baking powder into a mixing bowl and, using your fingertips, rub in the butter or margarine until the mixture resembles fine breadcrumbs. (This can be done in a food processor.) Stir in the sugar.

4 Lightly whisk the eggs with the cream, milk, peanut butter and vanilla essence. Stir the liquid into the dry ingredients, then add the chocolate chips and stir again.

5 Spoon the mixture into the prepared dish and level the surface.

6 Put into the slow cooker and pour in sufficient hot water to come halfway up the sides of the dish. Cover and cook on High for 3–4 hours until cooked through and firm to the touch.

7 Lift out of the slow cooker and allow to stand for 10 minutes, then loosen the sides with a knife, turn out on to a wire rack lined with non-stick baking parchment and leave to cool completely.

This is a wonderfully moist and delicious indulgence for ginger lovers everywhere. If you're not as mad about ginger as I am, you could replace the ground ginger with mixed spice and the crystallised ginger with the same measure of crystallised pineapple.

sticky ginger and walnut cake

MAKES AN 18 CM/7 IN CAKE

100 g/4 oz/½ cup butter or margarine, plus extra for greasing
100 g/4 oz/1 cup plain (all-purpose) flour
10 ml/2 tsp ground ginger
2.5 ml/½ tsp baking powder
175 g/6 oz/½ cup golden (light corn) syrup

100 g/4 oz/½ cup light muscovado sugar
2 eggs, lightly beaten
50 g/2 oz/½ cup walnuts, chopped
50 g/2 oz crystallised (candied) ginger, chopped

1 Preheat the slow cooker on High.

2 Lightly grease and line the base of an 18 cm/7 in ovenproof soufflé dish with non-stick baking parchment.

3 Sift the flour, ground ginger and baking powder into a mixing bowl and, using your fingertips, rub in the butter or margarine until the mixture resembles fine breadcrumbs. (This can be done in a food processor.)

4 Stir in the remaining ingredients, beating well.

5 Spoon the mixture into the prepared dish and level the surface.

6 Put into the slow cooker and pour in sufficient hot water to come halfway up the sides of the dish.

7 Cover and cook on High for 1½–2½ hours until cooked through and firm to the touch.

8 Lift out of the slow cooker and allow to stand for 5 minutes, then loosen the sides with a knife, turn out on to a wire rack lined with non-stick baking parchment and leave to cool completely.

Chocolate fans, especially adult ones, will love this surprisingly
light cake. It can be served warm while it is still soft, but I prefer
to enjoy it cold when it has set firm to a lovely creamy consistency –
though it takes a lot of self control to wait that long!

light chocolate and chestnut cake

MAKES AN 18 CM/7 IN CAKE

100 g/4 oz/½ cup unsalted (sweet)
   butter, plus extra for greasing
100 g/4 oz plain (semi-sweet)
   chocolate, broken into squares
100 g/4 oz canned or vacuum-packed
   chestnuts

120 ml/4 fl oz/½ cup milk
2 large eggs, separated
75 g/3 oz/⅓ cup caster (superfine)
   sugar
30 ml/2 tbsp plain (all-purpose) flour

1   Preheat the slow cooker on High.

2   Lightly grease and line the base of an 18 cm/7 in ovenproof soufflé
   dish with non-stick baking parchment.

3   Gently melt the butter with the chocolate in a pan on the hob or in
   the microwave until smooth and glossy.

4   Put the chestnuts and milk into a food processor or liquidiser and
   blend until smooth.

5   Beat the egg yolks with the sugar until light and fluffy. Sift the
   flour over the top, then stir in the chocolate and chestnut mixtures
   until smooth.

6   With clean beaters, whisk the egg whites until they form stiff
   peaks and fold them into the chocolate mixture. Pour the mixture
   into the prepared dish. Put into the slow cooker and pour in
   sufficient hot water to come halfway up the sides of the dish.

7   Cover and cook on High for 1–1½ hours until the cake is cooked
   through and pulling away from the sides of the dish (it will still
   have a slight 'wobble').

8   Lift out of the slow cooker and allow to stand for 5–10 minutes,
   then loosen the sides with a knife and turn out on to a wire rack
   lined with non-stick baking parchment.

PRESERVES

If, like me, you like to make small amounts of preserves, you will enjoy making them in your slow cooker. There's none of the steam that's normally associated with the process, there's no need to watch the pot carefully and there's little chance of the ingredients 'catching' on the bottom and burning.

In these recipes, the gentle, slow cooking produces the most delicious fruit curds, butters and preserves, as well as savoury relishes and pickled vegetables.

The citrus tang of this home-made curd is far superior to anything shop-bought. You can replace the limes with two more small lemons to make lemon curd, or with one small orange to make lemon and orange curd. Don't cook directly in the slow cooker as it will curdle.

slow-cooked lemon and lime curd

MAKES 1 KG/2¼ LB

100 g/4 oz/½ cup butter
450 g/1 lb/2 cups caster (superfine) sugar

Finely grated zest and juice of 2 lemons
Finely grated zest and juice of 2 limes
4 eggs, lightly beaten

1 Preheat the slow cooker on High.

2 Put the butter, sugar and citrus zests and juice into a pan and heat gently, stirring, until the butter has melted and the sugar has dissolved. Leave to cool.

3 Beat the eggs into the cooled mixture and strain into a 1.2 litre/ 2 pt/5 cup basin or soufflé dish.

4 Cover securely with foil and put into the slow cooker. Pour in sufficient boiling water to come halfway up the side of the dish.

5 Cover and cook on Low for 3–4 hours until thick. If possible, stir once or twice after the first 1½ hours.

6 Pour into warm, sterilised jars and seal.

7 Store in the refrigerator and use within 1 month.

The long, slow cooking produces a relish that is good enough
to eat straight away – no waiting for months for it to mature.
Don't be put off by the number of ingredients – it really is simple to make!
This makes a fairly large quantity but it will keep for absolutely ages.

traditional spiced apple and date relish

MAKES ABOUT 1.2 KG/2½ LB

700 g/1½ lb cooking (tart) apples, peeled, cored and chopped
225 g/8 oz stoned (pitted) dates, chopped
225 g/8 oz onions, finely chopped
350 g/12 oz/1½ cups soft light brown sugar
175 g/6 oz/1 cup sultanas (golden raisins)
150 ml/¼ pt/⅔ cup white or red wine vinegar
1 garlic clove, finely chopped
5 ml/1 tsp salt
2.5 ml/½ tsp white mustard seeds
2.5 ml/½ tsp ground allspice
2.5 ml/½ tsp ground ginger
A pinch of ground cloves
A pinch of chilli powder

1 Put all the ingredients in the slow cooker and stir well.

2 Cover and cook on Low for 7–10 hours, stirring occasionally after the first 2 hours.

3 Stir well before spooning into warm, sterilised jars.

4 Use within 3 months.

I like to use this in all sorts of ways, not just spread on toast but also spooned over ice-cream, folded into whipped cream or as a scrumptious filling for sponges and meringues. Don't be tempted to use the ready-to-eat, no-soak variety of apricots.

apricot preserve
with orange liqueur

MAKES ABOUT 1.2 KG/2½ LB

450 g/1 lb dried apricots
350 g/12 oz/1½ cups golden caster
   (superfine) or light muscovado
   sugar

30 ml/2 tbsp orange or almond
   liqueur

1   Put the apricots into a processor and, using the pulse button, process until finely chopped.

2   Put the apricots into the slow cooker and scatter the sugar over. Pour on 750 ml/1¼ pt/3 cups of boiling water and stir well.

3   Cover and cook on High for 2½ hours.

4   Stir the mixture, then continue cooking, uncovered, on High, stirring occasionally, for a further 2–3 hours, until thick.

5   Leave to cool slightly, then stir in the liqueur before spooning into warm, sterilised jars.

6   Keep refrigerated and use within 3 weeks.

This delicious spread can be left to cook for hours in the slow cooker –
I start it on one day, then mash the apples the following morning
before completing the cooking. Try leaving the skins on until the very last
minute, as this will extract as much flavour as possible.

slow-cooked spiced apple butter

MAKES ABOUT 450 G/1 LB

1 kg/2¼ lb Bramley cooking (tart)
   apples, quartered, cores removed
   and sliced
100 g/4 oz/½ cup golden caster
   (superfine) or light muscovado
   sugar

120 ml/4 fl oz/½ cup apple juice
2.5 ml/½ tsp ground mixed (apple-pie)
   spice
Finely grated zest and juice of
   ½ lemon

1 Put all the ingredients into the slow cooker, stir well, and then level the surface.

2 Cover and cook on Low for 8–10 hours or overnight.

3 Stir and mash the apples, then cook, uncovered, on High for a further 4–6 hours or until the mixture is very thick.

4 Sieve (strain) the apple mixture to remove the skins and spoon into warm, sterilised jars.

5 Keep in the fridge and use within 4 weeks.

You can substitute the vegetables suggested here for your own preferences. Serve them as an accompaniment to a plate of crusty bread and mature cheese – they will transform a commonplace ploughman's lunch into a tasty meal fit for the lord of the manor himself!

crunchy pickled vegetables in wine vinegar

SERVES 6–8

1 onion, thinly sliced
2 garlic cloves, finely chopped
225 g/8 oz tiny cauliflower florets
2 carrots, thinly sliced
2 small celery sticks, thinly sliced
10 ml/2 tsp sugar
5 ml/1 tsp ground turmeric

10 ml/2 tsp salt
2.5 ml/½ tsp freshly ground black pepper
2.5 ml/½ tsp fennel seeds
150 ml/¼ pt/⅔ cup white or red wine vinegar

1 Preheat the slow cooker while you prepare the ingredients.

2 Put all the ingredients into the slow cooker and mix well.

3 Pour over 150 ml/¼ pt/⅔ cup of boiling water and push the vegetables down in an even layer.

4 Cover and cook on High for 2 hours, stirring after 1 hour and 1½ hours.

5 Tip the mixture into a container, cover and leave to cool.

6 Chill until required. They will keep for 1–2 weeks in a covered container in the fridge.

INDEX